Can You Sing a HIGH "C"-
Without Straining?

Can You Sing a HIGH "C"-
Without Straining?

By Thomas Appell

VDP Publishing
17870 Skypark Circle, Suite 107
Irvine, CA 92614

1st printing 1992
ISBN 0-9632339-0-4

2nd Printing 1993
ISBN 0-9632339-1-2

3rd Printing 1999
ISBN 0-9632339-3-9

FOREWORD

I am a baritone, and for me even singing an "E" above middle "C" used to feel uncomfortable. I can remember singing in church as a teenager feeling my throat clench up at if I had to sing above middle "C." At that time for me singing a high "C" in full voice was impossible. I knew singers who could hit high notes. One of my friends, Owen Saunders, could sing incredibly high notes. I could only watch and wonder how he was doing it.

By watching and listening to singers like Owen, I knew there was a way to sing high notes easily without straining, so I set out on my own to discover exactly what it was. I took voice lessons from some of the best teachers in the world, studied books on singing, and did a tremendous amount of personal research using the principles of physics to figure out what has to happen to create a high pitch with the flexible mass of muscle tissue called the vocal cords. The research paid off. I knew I'd found the answer!!

I got so excited about what I learned through my research, I could hardly pass up the chance to begin teaching. That was 17 years and over 40,000 voice lessons ago. Since that time I've applied the same pioneering zeal that I had for discovering how to sing high notes to many other facets of vocalizing, and I've personally developed my full voice range to way beyond tenor high "C." At present, the average range increase for singers who train with me is 7 notes. Many get 12-15 notes of full voice range increase, and this book tells you how to do it.

I thank God for allowing me to uncover so many of the mysteries associated with singing, and I will enjoy sharing what I've learned with every reader of this book. You now hold the key. This book and the CDs and video that accompany it will show you exactly what you have to do to sing extremely high notes in full voice with no strain whatsoever. If someone with a voice as seemingly untrainable as mine can pull this off, you can too!!

Thomas Appell

PREFACE

Singing well requires a two-edged sword. You want to develop a solid vocal technique, a voice that is not limited in range or agility, as well as a sense of how to sing with style. Singers with great style and poor vocal technique usually thrash their voices attempting to sing high notes. Singers with great vocal technique who are stylistically sterile don't have a chance in a million to get a recording contract or succeed as a professional vocalist. This book was written to give singers an understanding of what good vocal technique is all about and show them how to apply good technique to songs with the kind of emotion and style that sends a chill up your spine and sells a lot of albums.

This book wasn't written to be the source of all vocal training for every singer who reads it. It is intended to supplement private vocal instruction. Singers who come into a voice studio armed with the information in this book will have a certain understanding of what to expect from a gifted vocal instructor. Great vocal coaches can have different approaches and that's OK as long as their objectives are right. At that first voice lesson, the student should hear the instructor saying he/she can learn to sing high notes easily without straining, every note sung in falsetto can be developed into a full voice, abdominal breathing is the correct way to breathe for singing, and that good vocal technique can be applied to any style of music. These are fundamental principles that need to be included in private instruction, and if they are not, you're in the wrong voice studio.

This book addresses head-on the most common complaint about private voice instruction...that you come in with a contemporary sound and come out sounding like an opera singer. It's unfortunate but true that many vocal coaches who really specialize in opera don't have the foggiest idea what a rock, pop, or R&B tune should sound like, but they still teach these styles. In this book I'll present a powerful method I've developed for capturing the most subtle elements of style in any song. You'll learn how to hear and note the things in a vocal performance that create your favorite singing styles. Teachers and students of singing who use the system presented in this book will improve their understanding of style and learn how to create it at the highest level.

The book comes with three audio CDs and 60 minute training videos for male and female singers. Listen to the CDs and watch the videos! Many of the things you'll read about in the book make a lot more sense after watching and listening to someone give you an example. The same video for children is available at the VDP Publishing website **www.vocalinstruction.com.**

A lot of the things I present in this book may seem almost too good to be true. Well, I've got some good news for you. It's all true. Under the direction of a good vocal coach, sopranos, altos, tenors, and baritones can all learn to sing extremely high notes... tenor high "C" and up, in full voice without having to go into falsetto and without straining, and almost anyone can learn to sing with a convincing style. I know, because I've trained hundreds of singers to do it. After you've read this book, you too will know it *can* be done!! And with training, you can do it too!!

I've included a number of quotes from students of mine in the text. The purpose of these quotes is to let the reader hear from someone else besides me that what is being presented in this book really does work.

Have fun singing!!

ACKNOWLEDGMENTS

Although I've done a lot of personal research about singing, God has always been the source of my wisdom, and it is to Him that I offer my deepest thanks for granting me the privilege of acquiring and now presenting the information contained in the pages of this book.

I also would like to thank three of the voice teachers whom I've studied with: Samuel Moore, Martin Green, and Roger Love. I learned much from these men and acknowledge their contribution to my understanding of singing.

Special thanks to Dawn Bullock, Lisa Guest, Patty House, and my wonderful wife Dianna for proofreading, Tamra Scott for word processing, and Brian Biolchino and Dan Parsons for page layout and desktop publishing.

Cover Design by Dan Parsons

Printing by KNI Incorporated
1261 State College Parkway
Anaheim, CA 92806

CONTENTS

PART 1

The Fundamentals of Singing

PART 2

Techniques for Training

PART 3

General Tips for Singing

Can You Sing a HIGH "C"– Without Straining?

PART 1

The Fundamentals of Singing

CHAPTER 1
So What Exactly Is It That Happens When You Sing?

When training your voice it's helpful to have a basic understanding of what is happening to create the sound. In this chapter I'll explain how sound is produced when you sing and what muscles are used to produce it.

The first thing you have to do to begin singing is to take a breath, inhaling air from the atmosphere into your lungs. After you've gotten the air down into your lungs, it has to come out in order for you to make a sound. On the way out, the air must pass through two small muscles in your throat called the vocal cords.

The vocal cords are located just below your chin inside an organ in your throat called the larynx. The cords are aligned side by side with one end affixed towards the front of the neck and the other end towards the back of the neck. The front ends of the cords meet together and do not separate. The rear end of the cords can be opened or closed for breathing and/or singing. The opening between the cords is called the **glottis.** By exercising the muscular ability of the vocal cords, you can squeeze the glottis shut, hold back the escaping air, and let it out in a controlled

FIGURE 1-1

The Vocal Cords (top view)

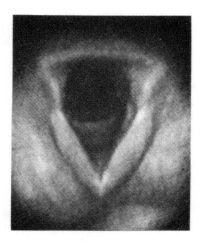

So What Exactly Is It That Happens When You Sing?

manner a little bit at a time. Figure 1-1 shows a picture of what the vocal cords look like in an open position while taking a breath.

As the air passes through the cords, it causes them to vibrate back and forth. This vibration produces the sound that creates your voice, and the frequency of vibration determines the pitch. With practice, you can consciously adjust the muscular action of the vocal cords to produce different pitches and vocal tone.

CHAPTER 2
Why You Can Play High Notes on a Guitar Easily

The guitar is an instrument that closely approximates the way your voice works. By understanding how to raise or lower the pitch of a guitar string, you can gain some valuable insight into how to sing high or low notes with your vocal cords. In this chapter, I'll explain how the pitch of a guitar string is changed and why high notes on a guitar string are just as easy to play as low notes.

If you were putting a brand new string on a guitar, you'd start by stringing it through the tailpiece. Then you'd wrap it around the tuning peg. As you started to twist the tuning peg, the string would get tighter. If you were picking the guitar string while twisting the tuning peg, you would note that the pitch of the string rises in proportion to the increased tension. If you kept twisting the tuning peg, the tension would continue to increase. Soon you would reach what I call the point of maximum comfortable tension. At this point, if you pulled the string any tighter, it would probably snap!! The pitch might have been raised a lot from where you started, but what if you weren't satisfied with how high it got? How would you get the string to play higher notes without pulling it any tighter?

You would just move your finger down the fretboard!! As you moved your finger down the fretboard, the portion of the string that's behind your finger wouldn't vibrate when you picked the string. Only the part of the string between your finger and the tailpiece would vibrate, and as your finger moved down the fretboard, (of the guitar) the distance between your finger and the tailpiece would shorten. *As the vibrating length of the string shortens, the pitch of the guitar string would rise with no increase in tension.*

Why You Can Play High Notes on a Guitar Easily

This shortening method adds a lot of flexibility to guitar playing, for by using it, the high notes on a guitar play just as easily as the low ones. In fact all of the notes on a guitar play with equal ease. The positioning is different, but it's not any more strenuous to play a high note on a guitar than to play a low note. That's a very important point to remember, because it represents a clear picture of what your singing should feel like throughout the entire range of your voice. High notes sing just as easily as low notes when you're properly warmed up and are using good vocal technique.

There are actually three things that determine the pitch of the guitar string: the length, the mass (thickness), and the tension. You can't change the mass of a guitar string, and unless you're using a whammy bar or bending a string, you don't change the tension. It's the length of the string that you usually change to play effortlessly throughout a wide range of notes.

All stringed instruments operate under the same principle. The next time you see a piano, notice the length and thickness of the strings that produce the high notes. They will be shorter and thinner than the strings used to produce the low notes.

Remember this one principle - when the tension and mass of a vibrating string is held constant, you can raise the pitch by shortening the vibrating length.

QUOTES FROM STUDENTS OF THOMAS APPELL

Kathryn Kukulka: *"Thomas is dedicated to seeing you grow. He understands how far he can push you which is usually much farther than you think you can go. Today's limitations become tomorrow's achievements. I think the most important things for the student to do is to trust the process (and Thomas), have an open mind, and practice. Students who can do these things will do things with their voice they never thought possible."*

CHAPTER 3
Why You Can Sing a HIGH "C"- Without Straining

In chapter 2, I explained why playing high notes on a guitar is just as easy as playing low notes. In this chapter, I'll explain why singing high notes can be just as easy as singing low notes, and I'll show you how to understand the way your voice works by comparing it to a guitar string.

When you sing very low notes, the vocal cords are short, thick, and loose. As you sing up the scale, they get longer, thinner, and more tense. When the cords reach their maximum length, an interesting thing happens. They start behaving a lot like a set of guitar strings placed side by side in your throat.

If you were going to raise the pitch on a guitar string, you would increase the tension of the string by twisting the tuning peg tighter. To sing higher, you increase the tension of the vocal cords by pulling tighter with the muscles on the ends. The tighter you pull, the higher you sing!! This tightening method works quite well until you pull the cords about as tight as they can pull without straining anything (probably to about an "E" above middle "C"). You can pull tighter on the cords and sing some higher notes, but you're not going to get very far, and you probably will get a hoarse throat for trying. You have to figure out another way to increase the pitch without increasing the pull. Here's how you do it.

Picture yourself pulling on the ends of the cords. Then take the muscles on the sides and start pressing the cords together from the back towards the front. The act of the cords pressing together like this is called **adduction.** The effect is kind of like a zipper gradually closing, and the result is the same as the guitarist fretting up the fretboard. Since the opening is smaller, the vibrating length of the cords will have shortened, and with no increase in tension, you will find yourself singing a much higher note. This shortening method is the secret to singing a high "C" without straining, and everybody you've ever heard sing high notes easily is doing it. They're all using the same technique whether they realize it or not.

Why You Can Sing a HIGH "C"- Without Straining

Think of these singers...Mickey Thomas, Ann Wilson, Brad Delp, Robert Plant, Whitney Houston, Mariah Carey. They all sing very high notes, and they make it look easy because it *is* easy. They're *not* straining. They're using this shortening technique. I have taught several of my voice students how to sing off the top of the piano after coaching them with this technique!! Almost every vocalist I have ever trained can sing to tenor high "C" (one octave above middle "C") in full voice, without having to go into falsetto, and without straining – baritones and altos included!!

To be a really good singer, you'll need to learn how to control the tension of your vocal cords. You'll need to know how to pull them loose or tight for soft or strong vocal tone. Next, you'll need to learn how to raise and lower the pitch of your voice by using the muscles on the sides to change the vibrating length.

Figure 3-1

"G" 1-1/2 octaves
below middle "C"

"C" 1 octave
above middle "C"

1   2   3   4

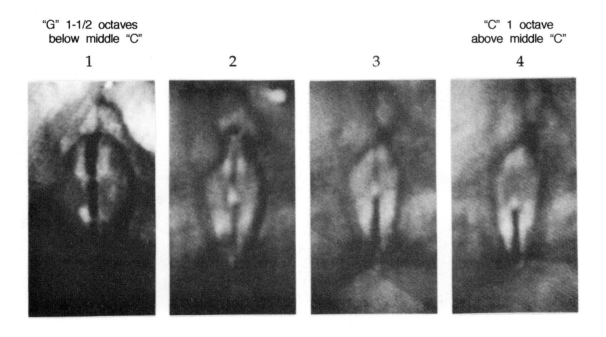

Can You Sing a HIGH "C"-
Without Straining?

Now if I were you, I would have just one big question. I would be thinking to myself, "Thomas, this technique sounds wonderful, and I can really see why it should work, but how in the world do you do it?" The answer is... found in the next chapter!!

Note: The action of the vocal cords adducting to produce high notes is a phenomenon I initially theorized and later verified through laboratory research. Working with a doctor specializing in speech therapy, a camera was suspended inside the throat of one of my students while we videotaped the performance of the vocal cords over a wide range of pitch. The photographs in Figure 3-1 were taken from the video produced during this experiment. The way of singing I am presenting is more than just another vocal "method." The way to sing a high "C" without straining as explained in this book is a physiological reality proven by direct observation.

Why You Can Sing a HIGH "C"- Without Straining

QUOTES FROM STUDENTS OF THOMAS APPELL

Kathie Schilli: *"When I first got to know Thomas, I joked about being able to sing a high 'C'. Thomas told me that if I stuck with it, I would be able to sing above high 'C' without straining. I practically couldn't believe him. But I figured, 'What the heck, I'll give it a try. What if he's right?' He was right!! More 'right' than I could ever have imagined. I've had one year of training and can sing to the 'A' above tenor high 'C' in full voice without straining so loud it almost hurts your ears to listen!!"*

CHAPTER 4
How to Sing a HIGH "C"- Without Straining

Since you can't see your vocal cords, you need to become familiar with the sensations that are produced when you're singing, and with how to control the cords indirectly by what you feel and hear. In this chapter I'll explain how to note these sensations.

What you hear when singing is a combination of the sound of the cords vibrating and the sound of the cords resonating. Where you feel the sensation of singing is where the resonance is most concentrated.

When singing a very low note, the cords are short and thick, and they will be vibrating along their entire length (see Figure 3-1, photograph 1). The sound will resonate below the vocal cords in the lower part of the throat and chest. The tone is characteristically big and open. Vocal coaches have coined a term for this. We call it **chest voice.**

As you sing up the scale, you'll start pulling tighter on the ends of the cords. As you pull tighter, the cords stretch. They get a little longer and thinner, but they will still be vibrating along their entire length (see Figure 3-1, photograph 2). The pitch rises because the cords are getting thinner, less mass is being used to produce the sound, and the tension on the cords is increasing. When you reach the point of maximum comfortable tension, the cords will be pulled as tightly as they can be safely pulled. To continue raising the pitch without straining, you'll need to start shortening the vibrating length by adducting with the side muscles.

As the cords adduct and the vibrating length begins to shorten, the glottis becomes smaller, and the sound begins to resonate above the cords in the head cavity. Resonance above the vocal cords is called **head voice.** The sensation of resonance will continue to rise as the size of the glottis gets smaller and smaller.

When the vibrating length of the cords is short, you'll feel the sensation of resonance above the cords in your head cavity (head voice). When the vibrating length of the cords is long, you'll feel the sensation of resonance below the cords in your lower throat and chest (chest voice). When the vibrating length of the cords is somewhere in between in size, you'll feel

10

How to Sing a HIGH "C"- Without Straining

the sensation of resonance proportionately high or low (a blend of head and chest voice...resonance above and below the cords simultaneously). What you hear and feel when singing is a small amount of sound produced by the cords and a lot of sound produced by resonance occurring above and/or below the cords.

An acoustic guitar works in much the same way. The strings don't really make that much sound. It's the guitar body amplifying the sound of the string that produces most of the characteristic sound of the guitar. The tone of the guitar has a lot to do with the shape of the guitar body just as the tone of your voice has a lot to do with the shape of the open space inside your chest, throat, and head.

While you're singing you can control the tension and vibrating length of the cords by adjusting the place where you feel the sensation of resonance for each note. For example, if you pulled the cords too tightly and strained while attempting to sing a high note in the first chorus of a tune, the next time you sing it you would put the sensation of resonance further up into your head from wherever you felt it the first time. This would cause the vibrating length to shorten. To keep the pitch from rising you would need to decrease the tension. The note would sing more easily.

On the other hand, if you sang the note too softly and wanted more power the second time around, the next time you sing the note you would bring the sensation of resonance down towards your chest from wherever you felt it the first time. This would cause the vibrating length and size of the glottis to increase. To keep the pitch from lowering you would need to pull tighter on the cords. As you pull tighter on the cords the intensity of the note would increase and you'd get your power.

In addition to making the sensation of resonance move above and below the cords, you can also make it move forward towards your nose or backwards towards the back of your head. Singing with the sensation of resonance towards the front of your face produces a "hooty" sound with a lot of resonance from the head cavity responsible for the overall volume. Singing with the sensation towards the back of your head produces an open sounding vocal tone with a lot more edge. Head resonance is kept to a minimum. With practice, you can learn to place the sensation of each note that you sing exactly where you want it.

Sometimes singers will tense unnecessary muscles while attempting to hit high notes. Students often "reach" for high notes by standing on their tiptoes, clenching fists, and tensing other internal muscles. I once trained a very beautiful female student who had this habit. During one particular lesson, her cords were adducting but not without some serious effort on her part. She was working hard, but not straining, so I kept pushing her higher and higher. In a classic attempt for the "G" above soprano high "C," she raised up on her tiptoes, grimaced, and then let out the biggest...errr...uh...well, I'll just say that she passed some gas in a very audible way. That was, to this date, one of the funniest moments in all my years of teaching. Moral: Don't tense unnecessary muscles. Use the sensations of resonance above and below the cords (chest and head voice) to guide your ascent to the highest notes in your range.

Remember, there are only three ways to make sound with your voice. There's the sound of the cords, the sound of resonance below the cords (chest voice), and the sound of resonance above the cords (head voice).

QUOTES FROM STUDENTS OF THOMAS APPELL

Mark Swoerder: *"Before I trained with Thomas I just sang 'naturally.' I now know I didn't have a clue as to the kind of muscular control necessary for a good vocal performance. My tone was airy, my range was limited, and I had a huge break between my lower and upper registers. I've learned how to control my voice, and I've developed a range I would never have thought possible without straining or harming my vocal cords. Don't get me wrong - my cords get worked. But I work them in a safe way that builds and strengthens instead of tearing them apart, which is how I used to vocalize before I learned how to sing properly."*

CHAPTER 5
Understanding the Break

Without training, most singers cannot sing a perfectly connected scale with no breaks from the lowest note in their range to the highest. Somewhere along the way they will probably encounter a point that will not connect. This is called a **break point**. It is also known as a passage area or the passagio. In this chapter I am going to explain why your voice tends to break when singing through passage areas. In Chapter 14, "Mastering the Break," I'll explain what you can do to stop your voice from breaking.

To achieve a perfectly connected scale without breaking starting from a low note, you would begin singing with the vocal cords pulled at a loose tension. To raise the pitch you would pull the cords tighter. As the tension increases the cords would go from being short and thick to long and thin. When the point of maximum comfortable tension is reached, you would begin shortening the vibrating length to sing higher notes by causing the muscles on the sides of the cords to adduct. This action would be analogous to a guitarist fretting up the fretboard.

It takes a lot of coordination to sing with loose or tight tension applied to the cords while adducting smoothly throughout their entire length. Most people have this coordination under control in the area where they've practiced it the most...where they speak. A break area often exists on the cords directly above that portion of their length that is well exercised through speech.

Let's imagine a singer with a speaking voice that normally goes up to "Eb" above middle "C." To produce the "Eb" while speaking, the singer has learned to adduct the cords with perfect control along the first quarter of their length using a tension of 6*. But at this point (labeled point B in Figure 5-1), the cords would resist further adduction, whether speaking or singing. From the posterior (rear) end of the cords (point A) to point B, adduction is easily accomplished at any tension, but from point B to point C the cords won't adduct at all, and from point C to the other end of the cords (point D), they will not adduct at vocal cord tensions above a 4

---

*Please refer to page 22, Figure 6-1, for an explanation of vocal cord tension.

(falsetto). If the singer wanted to produce an "E" with full voice, the tension would have to be increased to a 7 while adducting to point B. An "F" would take an 8; "Gb" a 9; and "G" would demand a tension of 10. At "G" the cords would be pulled as tight as they could be pulled, and attempting to sing an "Ab" would result in the cords jumping the distance along their length that won't touch, in this case from point B to point C. They'll come together again at a point between C and D that will produce an "Ab" with a tension of 4. Since there isn't sufficient muscular control between points C and D for the cords to adduct while being pulled tighter than a 4, the singer would get the note but lose the tension, and the result of the loss in tension would be a loss of power. The "Ab" would be sung in falsetto.

FIGURE 5-1*

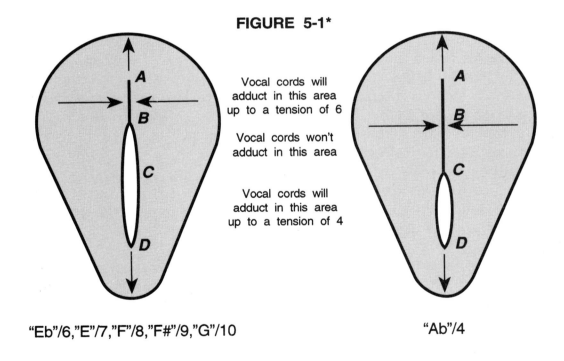

Vocal cords will adduct in this area up to a tension of 6

Vocal cords won't adduct in this area

Vocal cords will adduct in this area up to a tension of 4

"Eb"/6,"E"/7,"F"/8,"F#"/9,"G"/10   "Ab"/4

*Arrows in vocal cord diagrams represent the direction of muscular action. Arrows facing away from each other represent tension. Arrows facing each other represent compression.

Can You Sing a HIGH "C"-
Without Straining?

To help clarify the issue, I'll use the guitar analogy again. Picture a guitarist playing up the fretboard on the "B" (second) string. Placing a finger on the first fret, he plays a "C." The second fret plays a "Db"; the third a "D"; and the fourth an "Eb." To play the "E," he twists the tuning peg a notch, increasing the tension on the string instead of moving up the fretboard. He twists the tuning peg again to get the "F," again to get the "Gb," and again to get the "G." At this point, the string will not handle any further tightening. When trying for the "Ab" by tightening, the string slips from the tuning peg, the tension drops way down, and the guitarist has to instantly fret quite a ways up the guitar neck, say to where a "D" would normally be played, to keep the pitch up to "Ab" with the looser tension on the string.

Whenever you sing with your vocal cords adducted to just below a break point, they will resist further shortening. When you try to sing a higher note, the tension will increase, and your singing will feel strained. After jumping the break, the tension of the cords will be significantly reduced and the notes above the break will sing easily. The act of jumping the part that won't touch causes the vibrating length to instantly shorten and the sensation of singing jumps immediately up further into your head from wherever you were feeling it initially. This change in tonality is sometimes so drastic it can make you sound like two completely different singers. **An abrupt change in vocal cord tension will always cause an abrupt change in tonality.** The voice below a pronounced break is strong and powerful; the voice above the break is a weak falsetto. The term **lower register** is used to define the voice below the break. The term **upper register** is used to define the voice above the break.

It's important to note that the break in your voice doesn't always occur at the same pitch. Whenever you're singing through a portion of the cords that won't adduct, you're going to flip, and the pitch at which this occurs will be determined by the tension of the vocal cords. If you increase the tension of the cords, your break point will move up. Decrease the tension of the cords and your break point will move down.

Understanding the Break

FIGURE 5-2

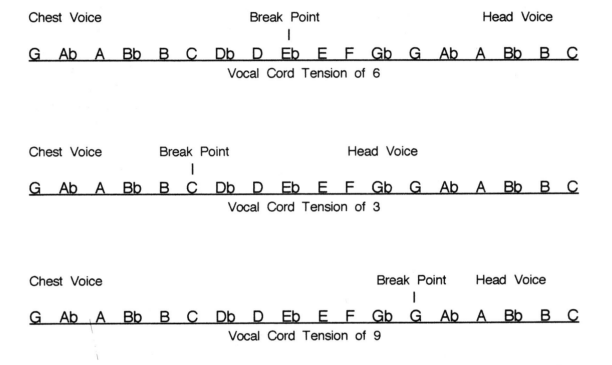

To illustrate, consider a male vocalist with a break at about "Eb" above middle "C" when singing at a tension of 6. Decrease the tension to a 3, and the break will lower down to about middle "C." Increase the tension to a 9, and the voice won't break until "G" (see Figure 5-2).

Can You Sing a HIGH "C"-
Without Straining?

This same principle applies to vocalists who have completely smoothed out all breaks or "passage" areas in their voices. Consider another male vocalist, only this time we'll give him perfect vocal technique. He has no breaks in his voice. When singing at a tension of 6, he'll note the transition from chest voice to head voice beginning to occur at "Eb." Lower the tension to a 3, and the transition starting point lowers. The sensation of head voice might come in around middle "C." If he increases the tension to 9, he may feel as though he holds on to chest voice up to about "G" above middle "C" before head voice starts coming in (see Figure 5-3).

FIGURE 5-3

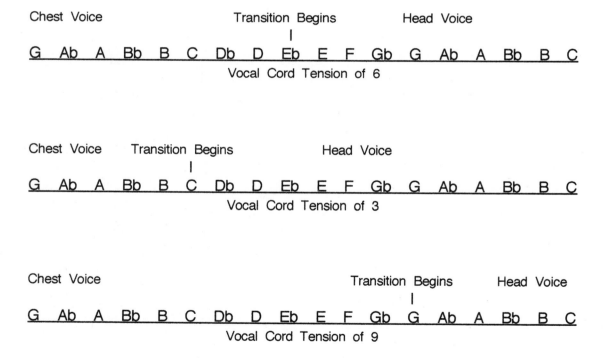

18

Understanding the Break

Some vocal instructors have suggested that everyone has three registers: chest, middle, and top or super head voice. While this can sometimes be true, it is not always the case. Some singers have no passage areas or break points in their voice, some have one, and yes, some have two (two break points separate the voice into three registers). In Italy, where the normal speech range encompasses very high and very low sounds, few men or women singers have breaks or passage areas in their voices. Italian singers have developed the ability to adduct smoothly throughout their entire range by speaking throughout their entire range. They've always sung with a perfectly connected tone and cannot understand how anyone could sing otherwise. Usually the concept of a "register" is brought about by singers who have an obvious break in their voice. I know, because I was one of them. I had two registers separated by a break that felt as wide as the Grand Canyon. I could not fathom how I would ever be able to sing across it smoothly.

Through training, I developed the ability to sing with no breaks anywhere in my vocal tone. As I slide smoothly from the lowest note in my range to the highest ("G," 1-1/2 octaves below middle "C," to soprano high "C"), it feels like one voice. Although I originally had two "registers," that feeling of having several "registers" or "voices" disappears when my technique is in good form. There are times when I have to work harder at maintaining a smooth transition, but when I am at my best, my sensation of vocal tone does not have distinct boundaries, although I do have general areas of sensation. I can feel low notes at the bottom of my throat close to my chest, very high notes up in the top of my head, and notes in between proportionately high or low. Like the singer illustrated in Figure 5-3, I can feel the transition between chest and head voice occurring at different pitches, depending on how tightly I am pulling the cords.

Sometimes when teaching I'll say, "Put the sensation more towards the middle of your head, or top of your head, or down towards your throat." My students know that I am just using the terms "top," "middle," and "throat" to describe general areas of sensation and not as distinct and separate parts of their voice.

19

Can You Sing a HIGH "C"-
Without Straining?

Many singers take a long time to smooth out their breaks completely, especially when singing in full voice across the most stubborn passage areas. Between now and when you have perfect vocal technique, there is a practical alternative. The next best thing to eliminating a break point in your voice is to raise it high enough so that your lower register encompasses most of the notes you would want to sing in full voice. Michael Bolton's voice represents a classic example of this concept. He's managed to work his lower register up to about an "F" above tenor high "C." He pulls a little tight at times, but he doesn't break— and he sells a lot of records. Britney Spears, Jewel, Celine Dion, Phil Collins, Bono (U2), Amy Grant, Garth Brooks, Sting, and Whitney Houston also use this technique. Actually, just about everybody uses this method that sings popular songs on the radio today.

Smoothing out the breaks in your voice involves training the cords to adduct (touch) where they won't come together. I'll explain how to do this in Chapter 14, "Mastering the Break," and how to increase the range of your lower register in Chapter 15, "How To Extend the Range of Your Full Voice."

QUOTES FROM STUDENTS OF THOMAS APPELL

Willy Williams: *"When I first started training with Thomas, I couldn't sing above 'E' above middle 'C.' Not in full voice, falsetto, or anything. Thomas showed me how the vibrating length of my vocal cords could be shortened so I could sing high notes easily without straining, and how to use my head voice. After he told me he knew I could sing a high 'C' if I stuck with the training, I got a lot of confidence. I began to believe that I could do it, and sure enough I can now sing a perfectly connected scale up to high 'C' with no breaks!!"*

CHAPTER 6
Understanding Falsetto

Many voice teachers, students of singing, and performers have discarded falsetto, not considering it a legitimate part of their vocalizing. I have never met anyone who fully understood what falsetto is, how it's produced, or how it should be utilized in training for singing. In this chapter, I'll explain what falsetto is and why knowing how to effectively control and produce falsetto is one of the most important skills any singer can have.

The origin of the term "falsetto" came many years ago from singers with poor vocal technique attempting unsuccessfully to cross their first passage area. Their voices were so strong singing up to the break and so weak singing above it that vocalizing above the break was considered to be "false singing," from which came the term "falsetto." Except for special effects, most singers began to think of singing in falsetto as a mark of inadequacy. Unfortunately, anyone who has discarded falsetto has definitely thrown out the baby with the bath water. The development and control of falsetto is a key to obtaining the ability to sing with complete mastery over the dynamics and intensity of your voice.

Falsetto is defined as a tone created with the vocal cords pulled loosely (below 5 on a scale from 1-10). Full voice occurs when the cords are pulled tighter. The tighter you pull the cords, the more air pressure it takes to make them vibrate. This increase in air pressure is perceived as an increase in intensity by someone listening to you sing. It's as simple as that. To help understand the relationship between falsetto and full voice, you need to understand how the tension of the vocal cords affects the intensity of vocal tone.

FIGURE 6-1

Vocal Cord Tension

1	2	3	4	5	6	7	8	9	10

Falsetto..................................Full Voice...

Understanding Falsetto

Vocal cord tensions from 1-4 produce varying degrees of falsetto. A tension of 1 one would create the softest tone the vocal cords are capable of producing. Tensions 2-4 would produce progressively stronger tones, but still soft enough to be called falsetto. A tension of 5 is in between - a little stronger than falsetto, a little softer than full voice. Tensions 6-10 produce varying degrees of a full voice. It's important to note that the intensity of the tone is a function of the tension only. Teachers of singing often use the terms "falsetto" and "head" voice interchangeably, as though they meant the same thing. They *don't* mean the same thing. "Falsetto" and "Full Voice" are terms that describe the intensity of the vocal tone. "Chest Voice" and "Head Voice" are terms that describe where you feel the sensation of resonance when you sing.

"Falsetto" is usually a term used to describe male voices, although it is equally applicable to female voices. The reason why males produce the most obvious falsetto is because they usually have an equally obvious break between chest and head voice, although many female singers also have a large break at this point.

Consider a male singer with an obvious break at "F#" when singing at a tension of 7. His chest voice just below the "break" at about "F#" is very strong and powerful. As he sings through the break area, the vibrating length shortens instantaneously and he flips way up into his head voice to sing the "G" with a tension of about 3. Since the breath support to the "F#" was strong, it's not uncommon for the singer to blow a lot of extra air through the weakly pulled cords and produce an "airy" tone. To the listener, hearing a focused chest voice 7 turn into to an airy head voice 3 sounds like the ultimate vocal cop-out. The singer couldn't hold on; he wimped out. Although the range of notes from "F" to "G" is a common place for singers to "flip" into falsetto, the act of going from a tightly pulled full voice to a soft falsetto can happen almost anywhere in a vocalist's range.

Can You Sing a HIGH "C"- Without Straining?

Singers are often counseled by their peers and voice teachers to never sing in falsetto. This is absolutely wrong. If you have a range of notes that can only be sung in falsetto, the solution is not to discard this part of your voice, but to strengthen it to be as strong as the rest of your range!!

You want to strengthen and coordinate the vocal cords to be able to adduct anywhere along their length while maintaining any tension from 1-10. This kind of training gives you the ability to sing in falsetto or full voice anywhere in your range. You don't want to lose the ability to sing with falsetto; you do want to gain the ability to cinch up the pull and glide smoothly into a full voice. For example, if you have a range of notes that you can't pull any tighter than a 3 in April, with training you might get them to a 5 by June and a 7 by September. When you've got the 7 under control, relaxing the pull back to a 3 or 4 or anywhere in between should be a cinch. It's the 7 that will take the time to develop. The strengthening doesn't come overnight, but it's definitely worth the wait.

Increasing the air pressure behind a loosely pulled set of cords produces what is called reinforced falsetto.* This increased air pressure will increase the volume of the vocalizing, but it does nothing for making the tone approach anything that resembles a full voice. Vocal students often confuse the feeling of pulling tighter on the cords with increasing the volume of the falsetto. This is where the guidance of a good vocal instructor becomes essential, especially when working on break areas above the octave above middle "C." In this region, you have to really know what to listen for to tell whether you're singing with a solid full voice that has a lot of head resonance, or whether you're reinforcing the falsetto which does nothing to help strengthen the voice.

Falsetto and reinforced falsetto are not "wrong" ways to sing. They are extremely useful as special effects in many fine vocal performances. Singers who have complete mastery over the tension of their vocal cords are able to glide smoothly from falsetto to full voice and back again with complete

*In classical music, opera, and conservative forms of musical theatre like *Phantom of the Opera*, all of the female singers sing all of the high notes in very strong reinforced falsetto. They're not allowed to use full voice at all.

freedom anywhere in their range. It's boring to hear someone sing with the same tension or tone all the time, and it's embarrassing to see a singer go up to a high note that he/she can only sing in falsetto. It shows class to hit a note in falsetto and then slam it with full voice a moment later. Colm Wilkinson gives a great example of this technique in his performance of the tune "Bring Him Home" from the soundtrack of *Les Miserables*. Singers like Colm leave the listener thinking they can do whatever they want to with their voice. And you know what? They probably can!!

QUOTES FROM STUDENTS OF THOMAS APPELL

Mike Ginty: *"In the first couple of bands I was in, everyone used to say 'The band sounds good, but the singer needs work.' I know why they said that. I sang all of my high notes in falsetto. It sounded fake. That was before I started taking voice lessons. After training with Thomas, magazines like BAM and Screamer that interview us after our shows are saying, 'The singer sounds good, but the band needs work.' When I am with a group of friends and I start singing along with the radio, if I really let loose, they just drop what they're doing and can't believe how good my voice sounds. I could never have taken my voice to where it is now on my own. It's the training that did it!!"*

CHAPTER 7
Understanding Children's Voices

Children's voices differ from adult voices in one significant way. Their vocal cords are shorter and thinner. I am baffled as to why more voice teachers have not figured this out. In this chapter, I'll explain some of the myths concerning the training of children's voices and present practical insight into how a child's voice should be developed.

The first and most absurd thing I have noticed about the treatment of young singers is that they are counseled not to train until their voices have "changed." Voice teachers who hold on to this theory must not have the foggiest idea of what happens when a child's voice changes. If they did, they would realize that proper training is the key to helping a young voice through puberty. I get so irritated when a parent tells me, "I talked with a vocal instructor on the phone yesterday and he/she said that I should wait to start my daughter with voice lessons until she's at least 13, so I am just going to hold off." When parents hear from a vocal instructor that it could be harmful to train their child's voice before it changes, it's hard to convince them that nothing could be further from the truth.

A child's voice "changes" as his/her vocal cords grow longer and thicker. Longer, thicker cords can hit lower notes. After puberty, the cords are long enough to begin sounding "adult" when singing or speaking. A child's voice will not change overnight because the cords don't grow significantly longer overnight.

When I was ten years old, I auditioned for a very good children's choir called "The Choralairs." I had near perfect pitch and a very beautiful upper range, and I got the part. It was a lot of fun because we got to sing on television almost every week and made a record album. I was classified as a boy "soprano." I am not and never was a soprano. The reason I was placed in the soprano section was because my falsetto sounded great and I didn't know how to sing in full voice!!

When I was 12 years old, my voice began to change noticeably. By the time I was 13, I was speaking much lower, but I always sang above my break point in what I now know to be a reinforced falsetto. At the time, I didn't know there was any other way to sing. I finally figured out by accident how to sing in my lower register, but because I had not worked at developing a smooth transition between my upper and lower registers, I had a terrible break point, and I couldn't sing a "D" above middle "C" in full voice without straining. My only alternative was to sing with falsetto. I ended up completely discarding my upper range (falsetto) and singing with a very limited range in full voice below my break point for a long time. I would have been spared years of strain on my throat and frustration as a singer had I been placed under the direction of a competent private vocal instructor at a young age before I had a chance to develop any serious vocal problems.

Some voice teachers would say that my voice changed at 13 when I discovered how to sing in full voice. This was not the case. My singing and speaking voice had lowered gradually as my vocal cords grew longer and thicker. The only reason my singing changed so abruptly was because I discovered that I could sing in full voice below the break point that had become pronounced due to a lack of training.

Like adults, most children have a definite break point in their voice, and prior to puberty it is also quite common for kids to sing only in their lower register below the break, disregarding their upper register (exactly opposite of the problem I had). When singing, they have to "belt" the high notes and can severely damage their voice at a very young age. I trained one seven-year-old girl who experienced chronic hoarseness and a limited range as a result of this phenomenon. Her cords wouldn't adduct under a tight pull, and all of the high notes she sang above her break were weak and airy. Her solution had been to yank the cords as tight as she could below her break to sing to her highest note, the "F," 1-1/2 octaves above middle "C." She couldn't sing in full voice or falsetto above this pitch. It took a year of weekly voice lessons to get her vocal technique in good enough shape for her to be able to sing up to soprano high "C" without straining.

Can You Sing a HIGH "C"-
Without Straining?

Kids can become amazingly good singers. I've worked with five-year-old kids who understood the difference between chest and head voice and could adjust the tone of their voice by raising or lowering their larynx. I've trained young kids who have nearly perfect pitch and very nice vibrato. I've trained several five-year-olds who sang a six-note arpeggio correctly after hearing it only a few times!! Many of my adult students couldn't do that!!

Recently a 12 year old girl I've been working with had a #1 Hit on mp3.com (the mega-huge music website) in the acoustic rock genre.*   In addition to getting e-mail from all over the world with new fans raving about her voice, the director of A & R at a very major record label contacted her and wanted a CD to review... all from one song.

The limiting factor with younger children is not their voice, but their attention span. They can begin training as soon as they can handle the discipline of a lesson, but it's important they train with the right trainer. Most kids who do a lot of singing are in some sort of school or church music program under the direction of a choir director. Don't think just because your child is in choir he or she is getting the kind of one-on-one training that will develop into a solid vocal technique. Most choir directors stick to choir directing and refer choir members who want to further their study to private voice teachers.

If there's one point I want to make in this chapter, it's that kids' voices are just like adult voices. If children are going to be doing a lot of singing, they will need the same kind of thorough training adults require. It's even more crucial for a child to have lessons because their reasoning isn't developed enough to know when they're doing something harmful to their voice. If you would like your child to have a good chance at becoming a professional singer, then I would recommend training to begin as soon as he or she can handle it. Why wait? Give them the edge!!

---

* You can listen to this song at **www.vocalinstruction.com** on the internet. Scroll to the page that says "#1 Hit Song CHANGE." There's a music video of the tune and a testimonial with the young singer and her mother.

QUOTES FROM STUDENTS OF THOMAS APPELL

Amanda Alexander (8 years old): *"I like you."*

Nina Espenousa (5 years old): *"I like the 'mi mi mi mi's' because they make me sing better!!"*

Cathy Rietkirk (13 years old): *"I am so excited!! Thomas recorded me singing a song he wrote and took it to a local radio station and they loved it!! I can hardly believe it!! It's been a lot of fun having my friends call up and request it so they can hear me on the air."*

Wolfgang Hagar (10 years old): *"I am a regular on the TV series 'The Wonder Years.' Recently one of the other characters had to sing a song for his part in the show. He couldn't sing it well enough and since the producers knew I had been taking voice lessons, I got to sing the song. Then he lip-synced to the recording of me on the air!! I would never have been able to do the recording if I hadn't been training with Thomas."*

CHAPTER 8
Vocal Classifications: Soprano, Alto, Tenor, Baritone

There are few things more misunderstood and misused than the common vocal classifications of soprano, alto, tenor, and baritone. In this chapter, I'll explain the true meaning of these terms, why altos and baritones have the most versatile voices, and why it's limiting to be a soprano or tenor.

For years, choir directors have branded male and female singers who couldn't hit high notes as baritones and altos. These unfortunate singers are often led to believe the myth that you are "born" with the ability to sing high notes easily, with full power, and without strain. I know this is true because I was one of them. As a teenager, I can still remember singing in church and feeling as if my throat was going to pop at "D" above middle "C"!! I sang in the church choir and got all of the low parts because I couldn't sing the high parts with anything but a reinforced falsetto. I was upset and frustrated that I had been "born" a baritone. As far as I knew, I would never be able to sing strongly up with the tenors. I am sure many altos reading this chapter have felt the same way about being able to sing in what is usually considered the soprano range. Luckily, I discovered the secret of how to sing high notes and can now vocalize over a greater range than most tenors!!

With this in mind, think back to Chapter 3 "How To Sing a HIGH "C" Without Straining." In that chapter you learned that the secret to singing high notes easily is by shortening the vibrating length of the vocal cords. Everybody can do this! Bass, baritone, alto, and soprano singers can all learn to sing high notes by singing with the cords adducted to a very short vibrating length. A baritone can learn to sing as high as a tenor, alto, or soprano if he wants to put the practice time in. If everybody can sing the high notes, then vocal classification must *not* be based on how high you sing. It's how *low* you sing that determines your vocal classification.

The length and mass of your vocal cords determines your voice type. Baritones/basses have the longest, thickest cords and can sing the lowest notes, often down to 2-1/2 octaves below middle "C." Tenors have shorter cords and can't sing much lower than the "A," 1-1/2 octaves below middle "C." Altos have even shorter cords and can't sing much lower than the "C" 1 octave below middle "C." Sopranos have the shortest, thinnest

Vocal Classifications: Soprano, Alto, Tenor, Baritone

cords and have a hard time singing below the "G" below middle "C." No matter how long your cords are, you can always shorten the vibrating length (adduct) to sing high notes easily without straining. But if you have short, thin cords, there's no way to increase the mass or length to produce a low pitch. Asking a tenor with short cords to sing as low as a baritone with long cords would be like asking a violin to play as low as a bass fiddle. It will never happen. For this reason sopranos and tenors simply can't hit low notes. They can only hit higher notes. Luckily for sopranos and tenors, most popular music written today is in a higher range that can be sung even if you were born with a set of short cords. Baritones and altos can hit the low notes *and* the high notes. I've trained countless baritones and altos to sing way past tenor high "C" in full voice. I trained one alto to sing off the top of the piano!!

A baritone came to me for voice lessons a few years ago. At his first lesson, he couldn't sing above "D" above middle "C," not in full voice, not in falsetto. He was currently one of the leading bass singers in the Orange County Master Chorale and had been for the preceding ten years. After about a year and a half of training, he learned to sing a tenor high "C," one octave above middle "C," with the sweetest most beautiful tone, effortlessly produced, that you could ever hope to hear. He auditioned for first tenor and got the part!! He told me that nobody could figure out what had happened to him. He told them he had just taken voice lessons, but they still had a hard time believing that a bass could ever sing tenor parts!! In fact, he could sing the tenor parts with more finesse and power than most of the tenors!!

Never forget, with training, baritones and altos can learn to sing just as high as tenors and sopranos. I know this sounds almost impossible, but it's true. On the male training video that comes with this book, the first music video shows one of my students singing the song "Wild Ride." The singer, Rich Compeau, is a true bass. He can sing two octaves below middle "C" with strong tone. "Wild Ride" is a pretty high song, but this guy just eats high notes for lunch. Have you ever heard the song "Barracuda" by the band *Heart*? It's probably one of the highest songs ever recorded for a female to sing in classic rock style. Rich can sing

Can You Sing a HIGH "C"-
Without Straining?

"Barracuda" note for note in full voice right along with Ann Wilson (the singer from *Heart*). Don't doubt it for a minute. Baritones and basses can sing as high as tenors, altos, and sopranos with proper training.

Some baritone/bass singers with exceptionally thick, long cords have a hard time learning to sing high notes in full voice. It takes longer to develop the coordination because there's more muscle to coordinate. They *can* learn, but it may take many years to develop. Be patient if you have to train awhile to get the high end to come in. I've never had a student complain about having a great sounding high "C" after they've got it – no matter how long it took to get. Some singers complain about how long it's taking, and many give up, not believing it will ever happen to them. Somehow, once you can do it, you forget all about the countless hours of practice required to get it.

Back in the California gold rush days an enterprising businessman purchased a plot of land in an area that seemed sure to deliver a rich vein of gold. He invested all of the money he had into this mine that he believed would make him rich. After several months of digging, they had not found any gold. They kept on digging, and digging, and digging. After many months of working the mine, they decided to give up, take a substantial loss, and sell the entire mine for a few hundred dollars to another investor. The new owner dug only a few feet further down the same mine and found one of the largest veins of gold ever discovered. The moral to this story... don't give up! You might be only a few days practice away from the increased range that you desire.

The highest note I could sing in falsetto used to be "F#" above tenor high "C." For nine months I hammered at that infuriating "F#," but try as I might, I couldn't sing a note higher. Then in *one* day while practicing I went from "F#" to soprano high "C" - a six note range increase. What if I had given up on those high notes after trying for five or six months? I wouldn't be singing soprano high "C"s today. Burn your bridges, don't look back, and don't give up - no matter how long it takes or how much practice time you have to put into your voice. Every single scale you sing brings you one step closer to the increased range you desire.

QUOTES FROM STUDENTS OF THOMAS APPELL

Mike Angeloff: *"I am an attorney as well as a professional musician. In addition to the responsibilities of running my law practice, I am either gigging or practicing five nights a week. Although I do have a busy schedule, I still find time to drive 75 miles one way for my voice lesson with Thomas. It takes me an hour and a half to get to his studio, but it's really worth the drive. I've worked with other vocal instructors, and they just weren't in the same league as Thomas. His teaching stands alone in maximizing my vocal potential."*

CHAPTER 9
Breathing for Singing

Most of the new students I train have never learned how to breathe correctly for singing. After I show them how, it's not uncommon for male and female singers to increase the range of their full voice by three or four notes - just by learning how to breathe the right way. Suffice it to say that correct breathing for singing is an important skill to develop if you want to be able to sing a high "C" without straining.

In this chapter I'll explain about respiration, how inspiration and expiration are accomplished, the three most common ways to breathe for singing (clavicular, thoracic, and abdominal breathing) and why abdominal breathing is the best method to use.

Respiration can be defined as a complete cycle of breathing, including inspiration and expiration. **Inspiration** is a term that means "to take a breath." **Expiration** is a term that means "to exhale." The lungs are the primary organs of respiration. Their purpose is to filter oxygen into the bloodstream from air obtained during inspiration.

The lungs are enclosed in a thin, flexible sac called the pleura. The sides of the lungs and pleura follow the interior outline of the thoracic (rib) cage. The bottom of the lungs and pleura conform to the shape of the top of the abdominal diaphragm. Air pressure within the pleura and lungs is very responsive to the movement of the thoracic cage and abdominal diaphragm.

If the thoracic cavity is enlarged by either a descent of the diaphragm or expansion of the thoracic cage, the pleura is expanded, air pressure inside the lungs lowers, and air from the atmosphere outside the body rushes in. If the size of the thoracic cavity is decreased, the pleura is compressed, and air is expelled outside the body into the atmosphere. By controlling the expansion of the thoracic cage and the descent and ascent of the abdominal diaphragm, a singer can effectively control the air pressure behind the vocal cords. Controlling the air pressure behind the vocal cords is fundamental to controlling the dynamics and intensity of singing.

CLAVICULAR BREATHING

Clavicular or chest breathing is identified by the expansion of the upper chest and raising of the shoulders and clavicles during inspiration. Air is inhaled by raising the chest and shoulders. This increases the volume of space inside the thoracic cavity and causes the air pressure inside the pleura and lungs to lower. When this happens air from the atmosphere rushes in. Air is expelled from the pleura and lungs as the chest and shoulders drop back down.

Clavicular breathing is probably the most common way for untrained singers to breathe. It doesn't work well at all for singing. Here's why. Go ahead and take a big, deep chest breath. Now exhale. Notice when you exhaled, you didn't push your chest down did you? You didn't pull it down either. You dropped it down. The weight of your chest squeezed out the air. You don't have muscles that pull or push your chest down. When you're singing high notes in full voice it takes a certain amount of air pressure to make the vocal cords vibrate. If you don't give the cords enough air pressure, you *don't* get the note. Unfortunately, the descent of your chest just doesn't have it. You could practice two hours per day for the next 20 years and if you were using this method to squeeze out your air you wouldn't notice one single note of full voice range increase. It just doesn't work.

If you see a popular singer use clavicular breathing when they sing, and they're singing high notes with some power, understand that they're using their abdominal muscles to squeeze out the air they took in by raising their chest. They would have an easier time sounding great if they learned how to use abdominal breathing to get the air in *and* to squeeze it out.

THORACIC BREATHING

Thoracic (rib) breathing is what most singers do because they heard from a friend who heard from a friend that when you breathe for singing, you're not supposed to raise your chest. Thoracic breathing is the worst way to breathe for singing.

In thoracic breathing, inspiration is accomplished by expanding the thoracic cage (the rib cage) near the midsection. The stomach is kept tight and hard. There are muscles that expand the rib cage to get the air in, but these muscles aren't capable of pushing the air out. Exhaling is accomplished by relaxing while the muscles seek to return to their original position. The action of the muscles is much like a stretched rubber band returning to its original shape.

Thoracic breathing doesn't work for the same reason that clavicular breathing doesn't work. You've got muscles that pull the ribs out to get the air in, but you don't have muscles that push the ribs back to squeeze the air out. So you can't generate enough air pressure to hit high notes in full voice.

Thoracic breathing is inefficient. Only a small amount of air is inhaled during inspiration. Singers who use thoracic breathing will find themselves running out of breath on phrases that they could easily sing had they taken an abdominal or clavicular breath.

ABDOMINAL BREATHING

Abdominal breathing is accomplished by utilizing a large muscle inside the thoracic cage called the abdominal diaphragm (see Figure 9-1). During inspiration, the central tendon attached to the middle of the diaphragm is contracted. The central tendon pulls the diaphragm straight down and the volume of the thoracic cavity is increased. This creates a vacuum inside the pleura, and air rushes in from the atmosphere through the mouth or nose to fill it up. The viscera (stomach and other organs below the abdominal diaphragm) are compressed and pop out as the diaphragm lowers. A protruding stomach is the characteristic sign of a well-executed abdominal breath.

FIGURE 9-1

The Abdominal Diaphragm

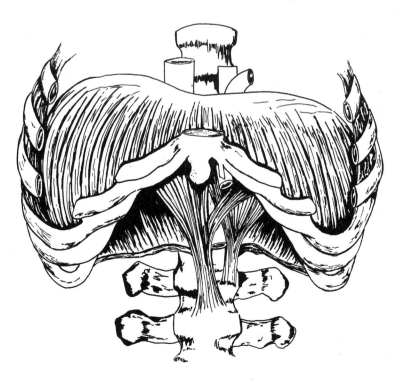

Can You Sing a HIGH "C"-
Without Straining?

There are no muscles capable of raising the abdominal diaphragm while exhaling. During expiration, the muscular fibers of the diaphragm are relaxed and seek to return to their original position. At the same time the muscular fibers of the pelvic diaphragm are firmly stabilized to support the compressed viscera which push the abdominal diaphragm up and the air out in a controlled squeeze.

While you're singing with an abdominal breath, it's easy to control the air pressure created inside the pleura and lungs, which translates into having control over the volume, dynamics, and intensity of the vocalizing. Abdominal breathing is lightning fast, extremely responsive, and easy to do. Also, since the muscles used for abdominal breathing are a long way away from your throat, after taking an abdominal breath, you don't feel any unnecessary tension in your voice created from inspiration.

During abdominal breathing, it's important to keep your chest and rib cage in a high but comfortable position. If you slouch when breathing abdominally, there's not as much room for expansion of the thoracic cavity, and you won't get as much air into the lungs while inhaling. If you're singing a short phrase that doesn't require a lot of air, you don't have to be as concerned about your posture. This gives you some freedom in your stage movement. However, if you're singing a long phrase that does require a lot of air, you'd better stand up straight before you take that breath!!

I have found that about nine out of ten new voice students, whether or not they've had previous training, cannot breathe abdominally without receiving instruction on how to do it. I am sure that some of them had been taught how to breathe abdominally by other teachers, but they forgot how. I usually give my vocal students 12 weeks of exercises to develop their ability to get a complete exchange of air with a nearly instantaneous abdominal breath.

Abdominal breathing is easiest to learn when you're lying down. Try this exercise. lay down on the floor, flat on your back. Place a phone book on your stomach. Try to inhale while pushing the phone book up with your stomach without moving your chest. Exhale by letting your stomach come back down. This is abdominal breathing.

Now take a watch and time the exercise. Inhale for four seconds, hold your breath for four seconds, and then exhale for four seconds. When you exhale, hiss with all your might. As you hiss, you should feel your abdominal muscles squeezing against the compressed air.

When you sing, you squeeze the air out just like when you're hissing, the difference being that your vocal cords are blocking the escaping air and not your teeth and tounge. You hold the air back in the same way that you would if you were making a loud grunt. The feeling is a lot like sustaining a comfortable shout, the point is to control the air pressure behind the vocal cords, and the results are amazing. I've seen countless singers hit a tenor high "C" in full voice for the first time within minutes of learning how inhale and exhale correctly using their abdominal muscles.

It's easy to learn how to breathe abdominally. Most singers can learn in a few minutes. It's hard to learn how to take a *quick* abdominal breath. Most of the 12 weeks of breathing exercises I give my students are geared towards teaching them how to increase the speed with which they take an abdominal breath. You should breathe abdominally whenever you speak or sing.

Can You Sing a HIGH "C"- Without Straining?

BREATHING TRIVIA

Singers who smoke can't hold their breath as long as singers who don't smoke. Smokers' lungs don't assimilate oxygen into the bloodstream as efficiently as the lungs of a nonsmoker, so given the same quantity of air, the smoker will feel starved for oxygen much sooner. Practically speaking, singers who smoke will need to breathe more often and will not be able to hold their notes as long as singers who don't smoke. Smoking also has a drying effect on the vocal cords which can make singing feel like a chore and cause a dry, raspy vocal tone.

The average volume of air that can be taken in during inspiration is 225 cubic inches for men and 175 cubic inches for women. No matter how hard a singer tries to expel every last cubic inch of air, there will always remain approximately 100 cubic inches of air within the lungs.

"Support" is a term used by many vocal instructors. It's a quick way of saying "the air pressure behind the vocal cords." When a vocal coach says, "Increase the support...," what he/she is really saying is, "Increase the air pressure behind the vocal cords."

In rare circumstances an abdominal breath alone will not get you through a long phrase on one breath. If this is the case, go ahead and raise your chest (clavicular breathing) to get in the additional air. I was producing a vocal session a few weeks ago where the singer could not sing through a phrase without running out of breath. We had tried enough times to know that she needed more air than an abdominal breath alone would deliver. After trying a combination abdominal/clavicular breath the singer sang through the line comfortably after only a couple of takes. Keep in mind that the only time to use a chest breath is when an abdominal breath alone won't cut it.

Sometimes when you're learning how to breathe abdominally, the extra oxygen can make you hyperventilate. I once had a female student pass out after doing some breathing exercises. She was standing in front of my

40

piano and slid right down the front of the piano and hung there by her chin!! Her eyes were wide open, and at first I didn't realize she was out cold. When she didn't respond to my calling her name, I rushed over to the other side of the piano and unhooked her. As soon as her chin stopped supporting her weight, she dropped like a lead balloon. Luckily I caught her. Now I know where the term "dead weight" came from!!

Guys can go down just as easily as girls. A few weeks ago I was training a teenage boy and he said he was starting to feel a little dizzy in the middle of a full voice exercise. He looked a little squeemish so I told him to start slowly crouching down so that if he fainted he wouldn't have too far to drop. Sure enough, no sooner were the words out of my mouth then down he went!

Most singers don't faint when doing exercises. These are the only two cases of fainting I've experienced in 17 years of teaching, although students do say they feel dizzy sometimes after their first or second lessons. Nervousness might have a lot to do with it, because the dizziness goes away in practically every case after the first couple of weeks when they get used to having voice lessons. If you start to feel a little dizzy in the middle of an exercise, *stop singing*. Try and relax, and if you begin again you might want to resume your lesson from a seated position.

QUOTES FROM STUDENTS OF THOMAS APPELL

Tish McGovern: *"I used to think that learning to breathe correctly would solve all of my vocal problems. It didn't. Abdominal breathing is the best and easiest way to breathe for singing, and every singer should learn how to do it, but it's not a cure-all. You could be taking perfect abdominal breaths, but if you can't control the action of your vocal cords, your vocal technique is going to be in serious trouble. Abdominal breathing isn't going to be the only thing you'll have to learn to be able to sing a high 'C' without straining. I learned how to breathe abdominally after only a few weeks, but it's taken a long time to develop the kind of muscular control in my vocal cords I need to sing well."*

CHAPTER 10
The Quiet Breath

It's great to be able to breathe correctly and even better to be able to breathe correctly and quietly. In this chapter, I'll explain the wonderful technique of taking a quiet breath.

Whenever you take a breath for singing, the amount of sound that you make is controlled by how tightly you're pulling on the cords. If you're pulling tightly, they'll actually sing while you inhale. If they're pulled a little, the sound produced is typical of what you would expect if someone asked you to take a breath. However, if the cords are relaxed, the opening between the cords (the glottis) is large (see Figure 10-1), and a breath is absolutely silent. It is also lightning fast because there is no drag as the air jets through a large opening. All sensation of breathing is removed from the throat. The only thing that you feel is the abdominal diaphragm dropping and your stomach popping out!!

Figure 10-1

The Glottis

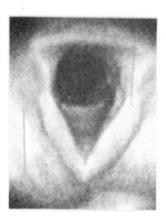 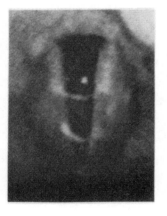

Open position for quiet breathing   Partially closed after singing,
                                            just before taking a noisy breath

The Quiet Breath

Quiet breathing is very useful for recording soft, tender vocal lines where a noisy breath might sound out of place and detract from the vocalizing. It is also a useful technique to use when a lot of air must be inhaled in a split second. Quiet breathing is the way to breathe unless you want to take a noisy breath for the character it adds to your singing.

Also, a general rule of thumb: When taking a breath for singing, always breathe through the largest opening. You have two options to consider. You can breathe through your mouth or through your nose. Since your oral opening is larger, you should *always breathe through your mouth.* Don't breathe through your nose when singing. The hole is too small!

QUOTES FROM STUDENTS OF THOMAS APPELL

Gary Klose: "Quiet breathing is so sensible, I don't know why more singers haven't adopted it. It does take a little time to master because you have to learn how to relax your vocal cords before taking a breath, but it sure makes breathing quickly a lot easier."

CHAPTER 11
The Technique of Exhaling

Have you ever been singing a song and felt starved for oxygen halfway through a phrase you knew you can sing easily with one breath? Your problem may not be with the breath you took to sing the phrase, but rather with what you're doing with the air left over after singing the previous phrase. In this chapter, I'll explain how you can get the most singing out of every breath you take. The secret is using the technique of exhaling.

Let's assume that you just took a breath for singing the first of two phrases identical in length. After singing the first phrase, you still have some air left over. That's good. You didn't run out of air and were able to sing without feeling starved for oxygen.

So you take your next breath. Now for some reason, the second phrase feels tough. You're pinched for oxygen after just a few notes. How come? What happened? The answer lies in the whereabouts of the air left over from the first breath that you *could* have exhaled.*

The second breath would have been smaller by the amount of extra air left over from the first breath. For example, if you used only half of the air taken in to sing the first phrase, the remaining half would be taking up space in the lungs. The oxygen supply would be depleted, so all that's left is stale carbon dioxide taking up valuable space that could be filled with fresh oxygen-rich air from a new breath. When inhaling, you will only get half of the amount you took in on the first breath. You will feel starved for oxygen much sooner even though you feel like you've taken a full breath. The solution to this problem is to exhale the air that you didn't use when singing.

Feeling starved for oxygen due to the presence of residual air is most acute when a short phrase is followed by a long one. Since you'll use only a small amount of air when singing the short phrase, you'll leave a lot of residual air. The residual air left over from singing the short phrase will

---

* After taking a breath, 100 cubic inches of residual air is retained in the lungs that cannot be exhaled. It's the residual air over and above 100 cubic inches that *could* have been exhaled that causes the problem.

greatly reduce the amount of air taken in for the long phrase, causing oxygen starvation.

Exhales serve a useful purpose, but they can also sound very emotional. Steve Perry shows off a great exhale on the tune "Foolish Heart" after singing the phrase, "We'll be there." Many of your favorite singers use exhales as a stylish and practical ornament. Add this little embellishment to your bag of vocal tricks. You'll be glad you did!!

QUOTES FROM STUDENTS OF THOMAS APPELL

Pete Owens: *"I used to get so frustrated when feeling starved for oxygen midway through a phrase I knew I could sing easily with one breath. After Thomas taught me how to exhale my residual air, I was able to sing through much longer phrases than ever before with a lot more control. The technique of exhaling to get a complete exchange of air seems so obvious to me now that I know how to do it, but I would never have thought about it on my own. I could have sung for years without figuring out why I always ran out of air. One of the reasons why I like taking private voice lessons is that I've been able to eliminate the bad habits in my vocal technique right from the start. I have a lot more freedom to sing without feeling held back by the things self-taught vocalists struggle with throughout their career."*

CHAPTER 12
The Vocal Fry

Brian Johnson, lead singer for hard rock band AC/DC, claims to have nodule-free vocal cords, yet his singing is characterized by hoarse-sounding screams that appear to be shredding his vocal cords to bits. John Schlitt, lead singer for Christian rock band Petra, sings with perfectly clean vocal tone on one tune, then crunches out the next with soaring, emotion-filled vocals backed by the sound of pure rasp. I can't recommend singing when your voice is hoarse or irritated, but by observing singers like Brian and John, I have learned a way to simulate the sound of a thrashed throat when your voice is perfectly healthy. It's called a **vocal fry**. When used occasionally, vocal fries can safely give you the sound of grit in your vocalizing. In this chapter, I'll explain how to create a vocal fry and present some examples of artists who do it well.

A vocal fry is accomplished by singing a note with less air support than would be required for a clean, focused tone. The vocal cords require a certain amount of air support to sing, and when they don't get it, the tone breaks up.

Vocal fries sound really emotional and kind of sexy, and they generally make a vocal line sound very convincing. Whitney Houston uses a vocal fry on the word "I" in the first line of the tune "You Give Good Love." A great example of a tear-jerking fry begins the phrase, "I love him..." on the last line of the tune "On My Own" from the soundtrack to Les_Miserables. Just be careful how often you use vocal fries. The key to detecting vocal abuse is hoarseness. If you start getting legitimately hoarse after doing a lot of fries, lay off the fries until your throat feels perfect. Don't sacrifice your voice for the sake of a few exotic tones.

Also, realize that many of the artists you hear on the radio have severely damaged voices. They have, in effect, thrashed their throats in order to advance their careers. I know that it's fun to emulate your favorite singers, but there are some singers that you can't sound like without tearing up your throat. Don't try. There's plenty of room at the top for good singers who want to make hit records using healthy vocal technique.

QUOTES FROM STUDENTS OF THOMAS APPELL

Marilyn Epps: *"Vocal fries are hard to do!! No kidding, they're a real trick to get right. It's easy to sound like you're choking or trying to clear your throat, but when you get a good one, it sounds really emotional. I've had to really work hard to get my vocal fries to sound convincing, but it's worth it because they add so much feeling to the songs I sing."*

CHAPTER 13
The Tone of Your Voice

A great vocal tone is one of the most important ingredients found in popular singers. The best singers have tones that are unique, captivating, and pleasing to listen to. They can sing almost anything, and you'd like it just because of the sound of their voice. Many singers don't realize how much can be done to improve the tone of their voice. In this chapter, I'll explain some of the things you can do to get a great-sounding vocal tone.

The tone of your voice has a lot to do with the size of your vocal cords and the shape of your head cavity. Long, thick cords sound deep and husky compared to the lighter sound of short, thin cords. When you sing, the configuration of the inside of your head determines what frequencies will resonate the loudest as your unique set of cords produces the sound. Since most of the sound produced when singing in head voice is from the resonant characteristics of your voice, the shape of your head cavity becomes an important factor in creating your tone. These physical characteristics will make the sound of your voice unique and original, because no one else has a set of cords or a head shaped exactly like yours. Some singers will have better tone than others because they were born with a better sounding set of cords and head cavity. That's the part of your tone that can't be changed. Luckily, there are plenty of other things you can do to manipulate the tone of your singing voice.

TONAL CONTROL WITH THE LARYNX

The part of the tone of your voice analogous to the treble and bass controls on a stereo is controlled by the position of an organ in your throat called the larynx. To find the larynx, just grab your throat. Now swallow. Can you feel something moving up and down? That's your larynx. The vocal cords are affixed inside the larynx. When your larynx is raised, the space above the vocal cords is decreased, causing low frequency resonance to diminish significantly. The vocal tone becomes thinner and brighter. When your larynx is lowered, the space above the vocal cords is increased, allowing low frequencies to resonate strongly. The vocal tone becomes deeper and richer.

The Tone of Your Voice

There is no such thing as a larynx position that is correct for all vocalizing. That would be like saying there's only one tone that you can use for every song you sing. You want to be able to sing with many different larynx positions: high, low, and everywhere in between – so that you can sing with an infinite number of tonalities and create the kind of tone that exactly suits whatever you happen to be singing.

Unfortunately, most singers have a larynx with a bad habit. It likes to raise right along with the pitch. If you allow this to happen, you may be singing really high notes in full voice with no strain whatsoever, but if your larynx is too high the tone is going to be really thin and whiney sounding. For this reason many of the exercises I give my students are centered around learning how to sing high notes with their larynx in a neutral position, not too high and not too low, for natural sounding tone so the tone of their voice on the top is just as rich as the tone of their voice on the bottom.

It can be a real trick to sing high notes without raising your larynx. There are two ways to solve the problem. You can try lowering your larynx down as far as it will go for the first few notes of an ascending exercise. It's still going to want to raise, but by the time it raises, with a little luck, it will have raised to about where you would have wanted it to be in the first place on the high notes. After practicing for a while with your larynx fooled into going to the right position on the high notes, you can try starting the exercise with your larynx in a neutral position and hopefully it will stay there.

Another option is to sing while allowing your larynx to raise. After you've gotten used to singing high notes in full voice with a high laryngeal position and the corresponding thin vocal tone, you can start trying to keep your larynx down while singing those high notes. Once you've gotten the cords used to singing a really high note in full voice, it's not as difficult to do a little laryngeal re-positioning.

TONAL CONTROL WITH THE VOCAL CORDS

Vocal cord tension greatly affects the tone. A tightly pulled set of cords has a lot of edge, power, and a very intense-sounding tone. Loose cords have a softer, more mellow tone.

The vibrating length of the vocal cords also dictates an important part of the overall vocal tonality. When you sing with a long vibrating length, and the sensation of singing near the throat (chest voice), a lot of mass is vibrating as you sing. The sound that you hear is a combination of the sound of the cords vibrating and the sound of the cords resonating inside the throat and chest. A small proportion of the sound is coming from the resonant characteristics of your head cavity. This type of tone is usually described as open or throaty.

When you sing with a short vibrating length, only a small amount of the mass of the cords is used to produce the sound. What you hear when singing in head voice is a small amount of sound produced by the cords and a lot of sound produced by the resonating characteristics of your head cavity. For lack of a better description, the tone can be described as "heady." Head voice sounds quite different from chest voice in much the same way that the sound of a guitar string resonating inside the body of a guitar sounds different from the sound of a guitar string played by itself.

TONAL CONTROL WITH AIR

The amount of air you let pass through the cords while singing is another important means of tonal control. If you sing with a very small amount of air, the tone will be clean and focused. This works great when you need to hold on to a note for a long time, but it can sound quite sterile. Generally, air in the vocal tone adds a lot of character. Check out the first verse in the classic song recorded by Celine Dion, "My Heart Will Go On," from the movie *Titanic*. She uses air quite effectively to deliver a gorgeous, tender, breathy tone that perfectly contrasts the blazing full voice she hits you with in the final chorus. I watched her sing this song at the Anaheim Pond here in California. You could have heard a pin drop in the middle of the 20,000 plus crowd during that first verse. I felt almost hypnotized. She had us dazzled, and she did it with air. You can't hold out a note for as long as when singing with a focused tone, but what it does for the emotion in your singing is well worth it. With a little practice, you can learn to adjust the amount of air for the tone you want to work with and the duration of the note you have to sing.

It usually sounds boring to sing with the same tone for any length of time. We like surprises and variety. Vocally, a song should have tonal differences that create a nice texture. Bono from U2 is a master at providing his listeners with a variety of tonal qualities. Check out the U2 tune "With or Without You." He moans and groans and uses air, falsetto, chest voice, head tones, cries, and vocal fries – and it sounds great!!

TONAL CONTROL WITH THE JAW AND TONGUE

The frequencies that resonate strongly when you sing are related to the configuration of the space in which they resonate. By changing the position of your jaw and/or tongue, you can change the shape of this resonating space and greatly improve the tone of your voice. Adjustments in the position of your jaw or tongue change the shape of the resonating space inside the oral cavity and can produce significant changes in the tone of your voice.

Many of the terms relating to tone can be very ambiguous unless you've heard an example of what they represent. You have to get to the point where you accurately associate the term with the tone. The video and audio CDs that accompany this book contain many examples of different kinds of vocal tones. Watch the video and listen to the CDs! Also, a good vocal coach will be an indispensible and helpful aide as you endeavor to understand the many tonal possibilities for your voice.

Can You Sing a HIGH "C"-
Without Straining?

QUOTES FROM STUDENTS OF THOMAS APPELL

Rebekah Fernando: *"Having great vocal tone is so important. My voice was especially prone to excessive head resonance, 'hooting' on high notes. I had to learn to really watch my jaw and larynx position when singing. If I don't have everything just right, it will sound bad in a flash. I used to get so frustrated during my voice lessons because Thomas would say, 'No that's not it. You're hooting again,' and I couldn't tell!! But after our lessons I'd go home and listen to the recording of the lesson, and it was usually clear what I was doing wrong. Thomas has taught me how to be acutely aware of my tone and how to keep it sounding right. Now, perhaps because I had to work on it so much, people who hear my recordings can't get over how pleasing my tone is. I can sing the simplest song, and it comes out sounding beautiful just because the tone of my voice has been so finely tuned."*

Can You Sing a HIGH "C"– Without Straining?

PART 2

Techniques for Training

CHAPTER 14
Mastering the Break

To master singing through a break or passage area, there are three ways to train, and train, and train. You go across it, through it, and strengthen it from the bottom up.

SINGING ACROSS THE BREAK

If you recall from Chapter 5, "Understanding the break," a break point is created whenever you try to sing across a portion of the vocal cords that won't adduct. By definition it is an abrupt change in vocal cord tension which causes a corresponding abrupt change in tonality. This exercise teaches the cords to adduct in the break area by repeatedly singing across it on connected scales and arpeggios.

When singing across a break point, each edge of the area that won't come together gets to touch briefly. In time, the muscular fibers at the edges of the break area, labeled points B and C in Figure 14-1, get so well

Figure 14-1

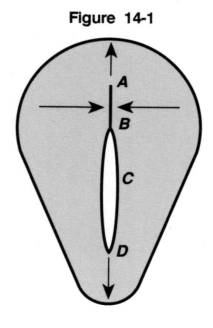

coordinated they begin to exert what I call a sphere of influence on the muscular fibers nearby, between points B and C. The cords will begin to adduct within the sphere of influence of points B and C, at first occasionally and later with more consistency. The portion of the cords inside the break area between points B and C (that is, within this sphere of influence) will eventually become as coordinated as points B and C are. As this happens, the break shrinks. In time, the muscular fibers at the newly shrunken edges of the break begin to exert their own sphere of influence. The process of shrinking the break continues in this manner until the entire break area is coordinated and able to adduct smoothly.

It's a tricky maneuver to get the cords to adduct smoothly while maintaining a tight pull on the ends. You will probably have more success with this exercise by singing connected scales and arpeggios softly with a loose tension on the vocal cords (3 on a scale of 1-10) at first. With practice, you should be able to develop a perfectly connected scale with no breaks at a low tension. When trying for a tighter pull, the cords will tend to break in the same place they did before. Then the game becomes trying to get the cords to adduct while pulling just a little bit tighter than a 3. When that's under control, you pull just a little bit more tightly, and so on, until the break area is completely coordinated at any tension.

I've noticed that it helps to lower your larynx when using this exercise to sing across a break area. Think of lowering your larynx the way you would think of using training wheels to learn how to ride a two wheel bicycle. As soon as you've learned how to ride the bike, you chuck the training wheels. As soon as you can sing smoothly across the break area with a low larynx position, try raising your larynx while maintaining a smooth transition. Your goal is to sing without breaking at any larynx position.

Most singers who have a pronounced break respond best by starting this exercise on disconnected arpeggios, using a consonant sound in front of the vowel on which to hop across the break points, moving the arpeggio up in half-step increments (see Figure 14-2).

Can You Sing a HIGH "C"-
Without Straining?

FIGURE 14-2

After you get the cords used to spot-adducting throughout their entire length on disconnected exercises, they will usually adduct with practically no break the first time you try a connected exercise. I also have found that humming on connected arpeggios across a break area is a little easier than singing with a vowel sound.

It can take from a few months to several years to iron out the most stubborn break points, so don't be discouraged if a smooth transition doesn't come right away. The important thing to remember is that it always comes!!

SINGING THROUGH THE BREAK

Most singers have a hard time changing the dynamics of their vocalizing without changing the pitch. This exercise teaches the cords to adduct through the break area while simultaneously increasing or decreasing the tension and maintaining a constant pitch. I call this exercise the crescendo, and I let my students begin using it after they've been doing connected exercises for a few weeks.

Begin the crescendo by singing a "B" below middle "C" with a tension of 1 in your head voice. You will be singing in falsetto with the vocal cords adducted to a short vibrating length. Your goal is to increase the tension on the cords to a 9 without breaking while singing the "B." Since you will be increasing the tension on the vocal cords, the vibrating length will need to simultaneously increase to keep the pitch from rising. The vocal cords will be forced to adduct in reverse right across the break area. As they do, each edge of the area that won't come together gets to touch briefly. The muscular fibers at the edges of the break area (labeled points B and C in Figure 14-3) get well-coordinated and begin exerting a sphere of influence on the muscular fibers nearby (between points B and C). As explained earlier in this chapter, when the vocal cords begin to adduct within the sphere of influence of points B and C, the break area shrinks and eventually disappears.

FIGURE 14-3

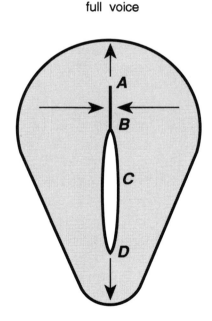

falsetto

full voice

Crescendo starting position
Loose tension; short vibrating length

Crescendo finishing position
Tight tension; long vibrating length

Can You Sing a HIGH "C"-
Without Straining?

The action of the cords in the crescendo is analogous to a guitarist increasing the tension on a guitar string by twisting the tuning peg tighter while simultaneously increasing the vibrating length of the guitar string by fretting down the fretboard to keep the pitch from rising.

As the vibrating length of the glottis is increased, the place where you feel the sound occurring will lower. At a tension of 1 at "B" in falsetto, you will start by feeling the sound in your head. It will drop down into your chest voice by the time you reach a tension of 9. Therefore, initially in the crescendo, you make the transition from the soft form of head voice known as falsetto to chest voice on the same note.

From "B," try the crescendo on succeedingly higher notes. When the starting note gets above a "G" above middle "C," you will notice that when going from a loose pull to a tight pull, the sensation will feel like it's going from a higher part of your head to a lower part of your head, rather than from head to chest. The tone will change from a light falsetto to a strong, full head voice, not at all like falsetto.

If you have a break point, your voice will flip every time you try to cross it going from falsetto to full voice. As the break area shrinks, the flip will become less pronounced. When your break point is eliminated, you can go smoothly from a tension of 1 to a tension of 9 on this exercise at any pitch with no break in the tone.

The coordinative effort required to increase the tension on your vocal cords while simultaneously increasing the vibrating length is quite a trick, but it really works great for eliminating any breaks in your voice. Since the crescendo works the cords in a different way than when you just sing across the break, when you combine it with connected exercises you will present a formidable assault on the most stubborn passage area.

A great variation of the crescendo is to go from a loose pull to a tight pull and then smoothly back from a tight pull to a loose pull – falsetto to full voice and back to falsetto – all with no breaks. I call this variation of the crescendo the "decrescendo."

58

Mastering the Break

Using the crescendo and decrescendo, you will gain the ability to sing with any tension, and you will have the choice of using a falsetto tone, full voice, or anything in between. However, when you do these exercises starting at higher pitches in head voice, you need to have a sharp ear to tell whether or not you're working the cords by trying to pull them tighter or just increasing the breath support behind a loosely pulled set of cords. Increasing the breath support behind a loosely pulled set of cords results in a reinforced falsetto and does not help to eliminate your break or build power and stamina in your full voice.

Many male and female singers have perfect vocal technique from the lowest notes in their range to about "F#" above middle "C." When I say "perfect vocal technique," I mean that they can sing a perfectly connected scale at any vocal cord tension in this range. At a tension of 7, a break point will occur at "F#," and the only way a "G" can be sung is by increasing the pull or jumping the break (i.e., decreasing the tension to about 3 and "wimping out" with falsetto). Continuing up the scale, at about "C" the cords will again experience a range of perfect vocal technique which may extend up to "E." Another break point occurs at "F," and singing above "F" is reduced to falsetto. The solution to training this type of voice is to work the area between "F#" and "C" and above "E" using all of the exercises in this chapter.

When singers of this voice type (quite rare) are singing up a scale and the voice flips or disconnects while going through a passage area, the singing on the other side is still "head voice." It's just head voice, or singing with head resonance at falsetto intensity. In the previous example, this stereotypical singer had the ability to sing with a full voice up to "F#" and then from "C" to "E." Singing with a full voice was not possible from "G" to "B" and above "E," which is where the training would be concentrated. Singers who possess this type of voice helped spread the myth that all voices have three registers.

Can You Sing a HIGH "C"-
Without Straining?

You will soon find that once the transition points in your voice are smoothed out, the trick becomes singing across them with power at tighter vocal cord tensions. I've trained some students who have learned to sing a perfectly connected scale strongly after training for only a few months, but others have taken several years to develop a workable volume using good technique while singing through what used to be a stubborn break point.

Trying to work out break points on your own can be accomplished. It's not impossible. It's nearly impossible. If you want to save yourself a lot of frustration and time, find the best voice teacher you can and take consistent weekly voice lessons until your break points are gone. Be prepared to do whatever it takes, and your break points will probably smooth out sooner than you think.

QUOTES FROM STUDENTS OF THOMAS APPELL

Clay Walker: *"I had taken a number of voice lessons before coming to Thomas, and there was nothing in the training I had received that dealt with smoothing out the break I have between my upper and lower register. After Thomas showed me what I was really doing, it was so obvious I was singing up to about 'A' above middle 'C' with decent technique, a little adduction, and then belting out the next few notes before breaking into falsetto. On my first lesson, Thomas immediately diagnosed my condition and began a very well-organized and systematic training program designed to slowly and effectively give me perfect vocal technique. Thomas gives me one-hour technique lessons once a week, giving each muscle just enough of a workout to strengthen and coordinate without overworking. It's the best and most comprehensive program of vocal technique I've ever seen and I would recommend it to anyone."*

Jim Owens: *"When I first started training with Thomas, I had a huge break between my chest and head voice. I can remember being a little shocked the first time I sang across it smoothly. I almost couldn't believe I had done it. It had seemed so impossible to sing a smoothly connected scale when I started training. I wouldn't have believed I could ever eliminate my break. But I had two friends who had trained with Thomas, and both of them developed a perfectly smooth transition between chest and head voice as well as an incredible range. Thomas told me it was just a matter of time and training, and he was right."*

Steve Mercado: *"Thomas has developed an incredible vocal technique that combines stylistic genius with an extensive upper range that's delivered with the cutting edge of a razor. It's an amazing technique that requires no strain yet yields such awesome power. After training with Thomas for three years, I was able to eliminate all breaks from my voice and extend my range up to soprano high 'C' with a full voice. It's no exaggeration for me to say that Thomas Appell is a true master in the art of vocal instruction."*

CHAPTER 15
How To Extend the Range of Your Full Voice

Singers have flown from all over the world to train with me because of the tremendous success I've had teaching people how to sing high notes in full voice without having to go into falsetto, and without straining. In this chapter I'll explain how to do this.

Recently a male singer came from Vienna, Austria to train with me for three weeks. He picked up 5-6 notes of full voice range increase in the first three days of training. This week a male singer flew here all the way from Japan to train with me with the hope of extending his range. Much to my delight, he sang his very first tenor high "C" in full voice on his first attempt after being thoroughly coached on exactly what to do. Five days later he was singing consistently at "G" *above* tenor high "C." Prior to reading this book he had never sung above a "G" above middle "C" in full voice.

A female country singer I started working with two weeks ago picked up 3 notes of full voice range extension after her first session and two more after her next lesson. The girl that you see first in the female training video that accompanies this book extended the range of her full voice by 15 notes in two days. These people are flying thousands of miles for voice lessons with me for one reason. They've read this chapter, done exactly what I said to do, and it worked.

For female singers in classical music, opera, and conservative forms of musical theatre like *Phantom of the Opera,* all of the girls sing all of the high notes in very strong reinforced falsetto. They're not allowed to use full voice at all. By contrast, in contemporary musical theatre like *Les Miserables* and anything anywhere on the radio, all of the really powerful high notes are going to be sung in full voice. Falsetto is used for singing softly and special effects (like yodeling), but it just doesn't cut it anymore for the main course of a lead vocal. You've got to be able to deliver the goods in **full voice.** Male singers have always had to sing all of the high notes in full voice, except (like for females) singing softly and special effects. If you have any questions about the difference between falsetto and full voice, turn back to page 22 and review Chapter 6, "Understanding Falsetto."

How To Extend the Range of Your Full Voice

There are three things you need to do to sing a high note in full voice. First, you need to take a big, deep, abdominal breath with your stomach sticking out as far as is comfortable and *squeeze out that air.* Do this...take a big deep abdominal breath. Now hiss with all your might. Can you feel your abdominal muscles squeezing against the compressed air?

Let me elaborate about how I want you to squeeze. Just pretend that someone was going to give you a punch in the stomach, but they told you about it ahead of time. The same way that you would tighten your stomach muscles to avoid having the wind knocked out from the force of the blow is exactly how you have to keep your stomach muscles tightened *every instant that you're singing in full voice.* When you take your breath your stomach should be sticking out. You need to harden your abdominal muscles while your stomach is pushed out. Don't suck it in and then try and sing. Keep it out. It should only come in as the air escapes through your vocal cords.

The next thing that you have to do is *block* **the escaping air by pressing your vocal cords together, like when you grunt.** Do this... make a loud, clean grunt. Can you feel something holding back the air? That's your vocal cords. When you squeeze from down below the air can't get out so *air pressure* builds up behind the cords. That's the pressure that sustains and creates your vocal tone.

The third thing you have to do is adduct the cords from the back towards the front, shortening the vibrating length to raise the pitch, like in the pictures in Figure 3-1 on page 7. As you do this, with each successive raise in pitch there will be more head resonance introduced into the vocal tone.

One thing you need to know about singing high notes in full voice - it's easiest to learn how to do this when singing really *loud.* The better you get at it, the easier it will be to back off of the intensity without feeling like you're going to flip into falsetto.

Can You Sing a HIGH "C"-
Without Straining?

The angle of your head to your neck *counts*. If you try to sing a high note in full voice while looking down, it's usually harder to do. Looking straight ahead works pretty good, and for most singers, if you angle your head up, it aligns the vocal cords to a position that makes the high notes sing a lot easier. Your goal is to find the optimum angle of your head to your neck for every sound that you sing. It may be different from sound to sound, and you have to experiment with different head to neck angles with each sound that you sing, and even with different pitches for the same sound to find out what head to neck angle suits you best.

Bending over and squeezing your ribs into your stomach area helps to generate extra air pressure. Many singers don't realize how hard they have to squeeze their stomach muscles and are not used to giving the vocal cords enough air pressure to sing high notes in full voice. Bending over is a great little trick to use to get those high notes to come out right the first time. When you bend over, don't look down. Keep your head up unless you've experimented with your head up and down and find that down works better for you.

To understand what the cords are doing when working on extending the range of your full voice, let's consider a singer who has a break point at "A" above middle "C" when singing with a tension of 8 (point B in Figure 15-1). From the back of the cords at the top of the illustration (point A) to point B, adduction is easily accomplished at any tension, but at point B, the cords would resist further adduction. From point B to point C the cords won't adduct at all, and from point C to the other end of the cords (point D), they will not adduct at vocal cords tensions above a 4 (falsetto). If the singer wanted to produce a "Bb" with full voice, the tension would have to be increased to a 9 while adducting to point B, and a "B" would demand a tension of 10. At "B," the cords would be pulled as tightly as they could be pulled. Attempting to sing a tenor high "C" would result in the cords jumping the distance along their length that wont touch (from point B to point C). They would tend to come together

FIGURE 15-1

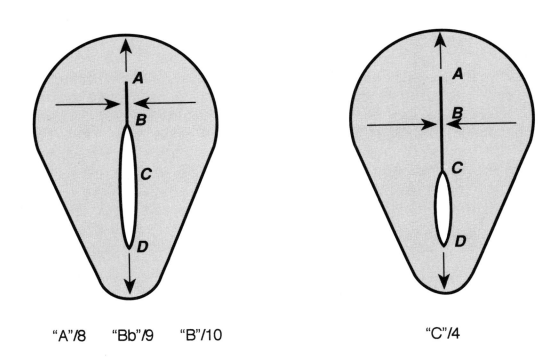

"A"/8   "Bb"/9   "B"/10   "C"/4

again at a point between points B and C that will produce a tenor high "C" with a tension of 4. The tenor high "C" would be sung in falsetto. This is the way your voice would tend to behave before training.

The muscular fibers at point B will exert a sphere of influence on the muscular fibers nearby. If the cords will adduct to point B where an "A" would be produced at a tension of 8, they can and will adduct for brief instances just a little further at the same tension to a point that will produce a "Bb." When training, you would repeatedly sing to an "A," trying to adduct one notch further without pulling any tighter. You can tell that you've got it right when there's a little more head resonance in the tone and the "Bb" sings as easily as the "A." **Remember, high notes sing just as easily as low notes. The positioning is different, but it's not any more strenuous to sing a high note than it is to sing a low note.**

Can You Sing a HIGH "C"-
Without Straining?

After you've sung an occasional "Bb" with good technique, the cords start getting used to it. Soon they become just as comfortable with the "Bb" as they used to be with the "A." Next you would try to sneak in a "B" by adducting another notch. When you've got the "B" you go for the tenor high "C." If you keep pushing the break point higher it will eventually disappear and you will be able to sing with full voice intensity throughout your entire range. This is how singers I train get 15 note range increases in full voice. Check out the introductory video that comes with the book. The first singer you see is a girl who added the notes from "Bb" above middle "C" to soprano high "C" to her full voice range - a 15 note range increase. She learned fast and got it all in a couple of days. This is not uncommon, but it doesn't really matter how long it takes. As long as you're attempting the exercises correctly, sit back and enjoy the ride. Whether it takes a couple of days or a couple of years, you're going to be equally elated when you can sing higher than most people can even imagine.

A lot of voice teachers tell their students to be satisfied with the range they can sing "naturally." This would be equivalent to telling a bodybuilder to be satisfied with the physique he or she was born with. They work their students in full voice up to where it starts sounding strained and say "Well, that's it for you. That's your range and you shouldn't try to sing higher because it might be harmful... and besides it's impossible to increase your range, so don't try..." Because these teachers don't know how to train someone to sing high notes in full voice, and don't believe it could happen anyway, under their training it probably is impossible.

How do I know this to be true? A good percentage of the singers I train have taken many, many voice lessons and spent thousands of dollars with teachers who have said these things. These poor singers end up with a strong lower register, a limited range, an obvious break point, and an upper register that will produce only a weak falsetto. Teachers of singing who don't believe you can extend the range of your voice have never learned to tell the difference between adduction and increased tension, so they can't direct their students to the right path. You could belt out high

How To Extend the Range of Your Full Voice

notes by simply pulling the cords tight for 20 years and never get one note of range increase. Teaching the cords to adduct is the key to extending the range of your full voice without straining.

When practicing exercises in full voice it's normal to experience some fatigue and dryness. Don't mistake dryness for hoarseness. As for fatigue, when the adductor muscles get tired they don't keep the cords together very well, the air pressure drops, and the tone breaks up into a vocal fry. This often happens midway through an exercise or song that seemed easy to sing at first. You might start out sounding fine, but after singing a few high notes in full voice the tone starts to break up and you feel like you can't hang on without straining. This can lead you to the assumption that you have made yourself hoarse by practicing too hard, or that your throat has been damaged.

While this can be true it is usually not the case. It's more likely that you have a stamina/endurance problem. The solution is to sing more high notes with just enough rest time so that your cords don't get fatigued to the point where they start to fry. If it's an exercise, sing one run and rest the next. Or sing one run and rest the next two runs. To develop stamina in songs a great training technique is to work up to being able to sing an entire song with a lot of high notes by starting out singing every other line. Then advance to singing two lines, resting one, etc., until you can sing the entire tune.

The first thing that comes when working on extending the range of your full voice is the range. For brief instances of time you will find yourself hitting notes higher than you ever thought possible with no strain. The next thing that comes is the stamina - strengthening the muscles to be able to sustain high notes without breaking up into a vocal fry. The last thing that comes is the comfort - feeling like it's practically effortless to sing.

There aren't any shortcuts to great vocal technique and developing the ability to sing high notes in full voice. You're going to have to work at it. The good news is, it *always* works. No matter how limited the range of your full voice is, it can be extended.

Chapter 16
Why Consonants Are Hard To Sing

If your vocal technique has recently advanced to the point where you can sing easily up to tenor high "C" in full voice, you may find that when you try to sing up to high "C" in a song, it doesn't work - at least not without straining or feeling very uncomfortable. The problem is probably with singing the consonants.

Consonants come in two varieties - voiced and unvoiced. A **voiced consonant** is one that can be sustained with pitch. Your vocal cords vibrate and create sound during the voiced consonant's production. With some voiced consonants the volume of the vocal tone can remain fairly steady. Examples are M, N, V, W, Y, and Z. **Unvoiced consonants** cannot be sustained with pitch, and the vocal cords do not produce sound during the unvoiced consonant's production. Examples are S and F. With some unvoiced consonants, the air flow through the cords is stopped completely for an instant. Examples are T, K, and P.

There are two reasons why it's hard to sing consonants on a high note in full voice. The first reason is because *the muscles used to form the consonant affect the control of the muscles used to make the vocal cords hit the high note.* Let me show you what I mean. Try moving the middle toe on your left foot without moving the others. Can't do it? You have the muscles necessary to move all of your toes independently, but you won't be able to control them one at a time unless you practice. When you try to curl one toe, they all will want to curl.

Your vocal cords work in the same way. The vocal cords are a muscle, and are affected by the muscles that move your tongue, jaw, and mouth. When you try to pronounce a consonant like K, you have to pull your tongue towards the roof of your mouth. The small movement of the muscle that raises your tongue has a big effect on the cords adducting properly to sing in a higher range. I have many students who can sing a perfect tenor high "C" in full voice on almost any vowel sound, but can't sing comfortably above a "G" above middle "C" in a song because of the consonants.

Why Consonants Are Hard To Sing

The second reason why it's difficult to sing a consonant on a high note in full voice is because *the vocal tone is interrupted.* Voiced consonants aren't that hard to sing because with practice you can learn to maintain a fairly steady vocal tone. Unvoiced consonants are difficult to sing because the cords have to stop producing sound and then start up again from scratch with the right pitch and intensity. Each time the cords stop producing sound, they tend to forget the position they were in while hitting the note. This would be analogous to a guitarist fingering a difficult cord, and in between strums having to take his fingers completely off of the fretboard, and then re-position them perfectly in time for the next strum.

For example, say the word kite three times in a row. Did you notice how each time you pronounce the K, the sound stops for an instant? Now try singing the word kite three times in a row in full voice on middle "C." Not too bad. Now try singing it in full voice on "G" above middle "C." Getting tougher. Now try singing the word kite three times in a row in full voice as close to tenor high "C" as you can get. Unless you have a very smart throat, singing a tenor high "C" on any unvoiced consonant will feel uncomfortable. You have to train the cords to be able to stop vibrating for an instant, sing a consonant, and then go right back to producing the tone you want.

Singing low notes and singing in falsetto is easier to do with un-voiced consonants. Singing unvoiced consonants in full voice on high notes will be toughest. The tighter the tension on the vocal cords, the more susceptible your singing will be to influence from a voiced or unvoiced consonant.

You can learn to sing voiced and unvoiced consonants in full voice on high notes by practicing vocal exercises...scales and arpeggios seasoned with your favorite consonant. It's also a lot of fun to use songs for working on consonants. I use many songs as exercises for my students, picking songs that are just barely attainable for them to sing in full voice. After a few weeks of practicing with the tune, the student is almost always ready for a new song to work on with higher notes in full voice.

Can You Sing a HIGH "C"-
Without Straining?

There's no doubt about it - learning how to sing in full voice on high notes in a song is tough (because of the consonants), but if you stick with consistent exercising and lots of song-work in full voice, even the most difficult songs will become routinely attainable.

At the World Music Awards in 1999, Cher, the near-icon status singer and actress, was chosen to close the show by singing one of her recent hit songs. After singing she addressed the audience and said... *"God must have some kind of a sense of humor to let me do all of the things I've done - sell a lot of records and make lots of money. But if there's one thought I'd like to leave you with, it's this. Don't give up. Hold on to your dreams, and if you just don't give up trying they'll probably become real."*

Don't give up! Listen to the words of someone who's been there and done it. Superstar status doesn't come to the lazy, It doesn't come to those who fall apart after their first criticism. It comes to those who refuse to accept anything less than the exact fullfilment of their dream.

If your dream is to become a great singer, do everything you can to make your dream a reality. With God's help and a fierce determination on your part, your dream *can* become a reality.

Why Consonants Are Hard To Sing

QUOTES FROM STUDENTS OF THOMAS APPELL

Rohn Puckett: *"Those #%?!! consonants frustrate me like nothing else. I can sing up to 'F' above tenor high 'C' in full voice, but I often choke on 'A' below tenor high 'C' in my songs because of having to sing the consonants. I have to really concentrate to keep my cords working properly while my mouth, tongue, and jaw change positions to form the consonants. Singing lots of songs in full voice is the best way I've found to improve this part of my vocal technique."*

CHAPTER 17
How To Develop Vibrato

When I first started teaching, I remember training a young fifteen-year-old girl named Angie. We had worked on vocal technique for a few months, and she was improving, but compared to some of my other students, she didn't sound overly impressive – at least not yet. Then one day during a lesson, she told me about a performance she had coming up and asked if we could begin working on the song she wanted to sing. Her technique was coming along nicely, so I agreed. At the next lesson I started by having her sing the song she had chosen with an accompaniment track.

I was practically speechless after her performance. She sounded so good it practically brought tears to my eyes. But the only thing she added to her average vocal technique was vibrato. I never forgot that lesson. I thought of all the other students I had who couldn't sing with vibrato at all and how much better they would sound if I could somehow teach them how to do it. Then I thought of the students I had who had developed a vibrato quality so annoying they would probably sound better without it. I decided then and there that I was going to find out everything I could about how vibrato is produced, what qualities make it sound great, and what qualities make it sound bad.

After many years of study and listening to hundreds of singers with excellent vibrato, I have learned how to teach just about anyone how to develop great vibrato through training. In this chapter, I am going to explain the three different ways to produce vibrato and present some exercises for developing it.

There are three ways of creating vibrato when singing. You can use pitch variation, pulsing, or tonal variation.

PITCH VARIATION

Pitch variation occurs when the pitch of the vocal tone goes up and down at a constant volume (see Figure 17-1). This is the kind of vibrato used by violinists when they rock their finger back and forth on the string. Usually vibrato with pitch variation has a smooth, flowing feel to it.

FIGURE 17-1

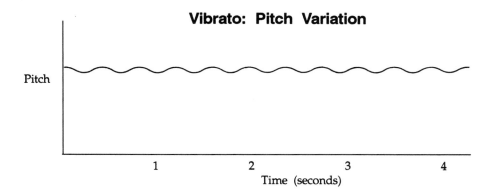

PULSING

Pulsing occurs when the volume of the vocal tone goes up and down at a constant pitch (see Figure 17-2). This effect sounds a lot like taking the volume control of an electric guitar, playing a note, then twisting it down and up, down and up, over and over. A strong pulse lends more of a choppy feel to the vibrato quality.

FIGURE 17-2

Vibrato: Pulsing

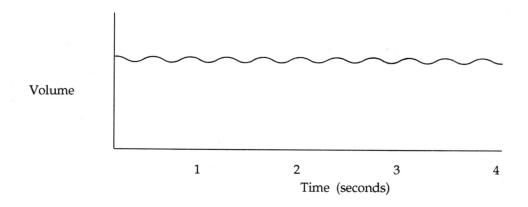

CHAPTER 17
How to Develop Vibrato

TONAL VARIATION

Tonal variation is accomplished by moving your jaw up and down in sync with the pitch variation and/or pulsing. The jaw movement changes the tone of the vowel sound and adds a smooth, pleasing effect to the vibrato quality. It also helps to keep the timing of your vibes even, kind of like tapping your foot. I have noticed that the very best singers seem to use tonal variation quite often.

There is a fourth variable in the vibrato quality – the speed. You can speed the vibrato up or slow it down. You can also increase or decrease the depth of the pitch variation and/or pulsing to exaggerate the overall vibrato effect.

When producing vibrato, you can have pulsing, pitch, and tonal variation happening simultaneously or by themselves to create many interesting vibrato qualities.

Often during a first voice lesson, I'll hear a student producing an uncontrolled flutter. Upon questioning, they often respond by saying they thought they were producing vibrato. They were. It's just that uncontrolled, uneven, fluttery vibrato sounds bad and detracts from the singing. Many of the students who come to me for training have developed a vibrato with a "bug" in it. There is something in the vibrato quality that would be unlikely to surface in a hit record. My job is to identify the "bug" and work it out through exercising.

Normally, vibrato is difficult to do evenly at faster rates. For this reason, when training, you should start at slower speeds and work your way up to the faster ones. I have developed some excellent exercises for this purpose.

Can You Sing a HIGH "C"- Without Straining?

Vibrato Exercise #1
PITCH VARIATION

For this exercise, the goal is to slide smoothly from the top note of a minor third to the bottom note with no break at a constant volume. Begin at a metronome setting of 100 for each quarter note. When you can do the exercise perfectly at 100, advance to the next higher speed on the metronome. When you reach 160, go to Vibrato Exercise #2.

Vibrato Exercise #2
PITCH VARIATION

The objective of this exercise is the same as in Vibrato Exercise #1. Only the interval has been changed. Hit the top note and the bottom note of a whole step interval and slide smoothly in between at a constant volume. You should start at a metronome setting of 80 for each eighth note and take it up to about 112. You can also do this exercise with a half-step interval.

How to Develop Vibrato

Vibrato Exercise #3
PULSING

The objective of this exercise is to create a smooth pulse. A pulse can be created by going from a higher volume to a lower volume and back again while maintaining a constant pitch. Begin the exercise at a metronome setting of 168 and do one pulse per beat with the higher volume on the beat. Nodding your head in sync with the metronome really helps. The down motion of your head would be on the beat. Do this exercise in groups of eight: seven beats of pulsing and one beat to take a breath. Start singing at "A" below middle "C" and move up one half-step each time you finish a group of eight pulses. Sing up to an octave above middle "C" and then come back down. After you feel comfortable with the exercise, start at a lower note and sing to a higher note if you can. When you have mastered a smooth pulse at 168, go to Vibrato Exercises #4, #5, and #6.

Vibrato Exercise #4
PULSING

Begin this exercise at a metronome setting of 100 and do two vibes per beat. You can still do groups of eight beats. I say "vibes" because at this point it's OK to start adding a little pitch variation to the vibrato quality. You don't need to do a strict pulse. Just be sure to have some pulse in the vibrato quality. I usually work out my students to about 160 on this exercise.

Vibrato Exercise #5
PULSING

Begin this exercise at a metronome setting of 76 and do three vibes per beat. I usually work out my students to about 112.

Vibrato Exercise #6
PULSING

Begin this exercise at a metronome setting of 60 for each eighth note and do four vibes per beat. I usually work out my students to about 84.

VIBRATO FADE-INS

When a singer has to hold out a note for a long time, it can sound too "operatic" to have vibrato going the entire time. The solution is to do what is called a vibrato fade-in (see figure 17-3). You sing straight with no vibes for a while and then smoothly fade in vibrato by gradually increasing the depth until after a few counts, it is fully developed.

FIGURE 17-3

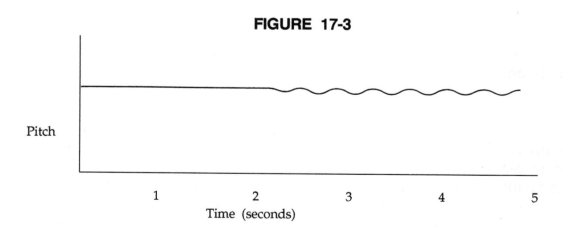

How to Develop Vibrato

Vibrato fade-ins sound really stylish and do a lot for spicing up potentially uneventful notes. To practice fade-ins, use the format for all of the pulsing exercises, but instead of singing with vibrato the entire time, in an eight-count exercise, start by doing one count straight, the rest with vibes, then two counts straight, the rest with vibes, and so on. When you get to eight counts straight, sing with absolutely no vibrato for the entire exercise. It's good practice to train the cords to hold out a perfectly straight tone.

Most of the singers who have great vibes learned how to produce vibrato by emulating their favorite artists. It takes a long time to get good vibes this way, but it works. Unfortunately, most singers have a hard time developing good vibrato through emulation. They honestly can't tell when their vibes sound terrible. I have found that nine out of ten singers who come to me for training have poor vibrato, do not know how to improve or develop vibrato on their own, and have a hard time learning how to recognize what good vibrato sounds like in the first place. For example, vibrato can be uneven in several different ways. It's usually obvious if the timing is haphazard. But it's not uncommon to find a singer with a good sense of timing who has trouble keeping the depth of the pitch variation or the pulse constant. An untrained ear might just hear the resultant vibrato and not like it but not know why. You really have to know what to look for to hear these split-second irregularities. Keep in mind that vibrato usually sounds best when it is fairly uniform in all respects. If the depth of the pitch variation or the pulse does change, it should change smoothly enough to not appear like a mistake.

Vibrato can be overused. Some singers sound like they turned their vibrato switch on full and forgot about it. If you want to please a younger audience (age 50 and below), you'd better learn how to turn off your vibes. On the other hand, singing without vibrato on classically oriented songs can sound equally out of place. Vibrato can be overdone. Excessive vibrato depth leads to an operatic quality that would kill a pop tune. Vibrato can be too even, too perfect, like a drum machine that leaves you longing for the subtle changes inherent to real drumming. This problem is especially prone to occur on longer notes. The solution is to smoothly vary the pitch variation and/or pulse randomly to create an uneven vibrato that still sounds right to the ear. I might add here that you have to be a really good singer to produce uneven vibrato and have it come out sounding decent.

I have found that beginning singers need to plan where they place vibrato a lot more than experienced vocalists who can go by feel and have it come out right. If you can't sing from your soul and have your vibrato sound wonderful, you probably should do a little more planning. It's not bad to plan either. Often when I am working out a vocal line with strict timing and an even feel, I'll actually count the vibes I place on key words. If you do it right, it never sounds phony.

A lot of voice teachers hear the vibrato as a single entity. I hear six different characteristics of vibrato occurring simultaneously: pitch variation, pulsing, tonal variation, speed, depth, and evenness. Usually if one of them sounds "wrong," I can sense it... and "wrong" does not always mean not perfect. Sometimes "wrong" is too perfect. If you're going to teach vibrato development, you have to listen to a lot of great singers to find out what qualities you like or dislike about their vibrato. Being able to hear – and I mean really hear – all of the characteristics that comprise good sounding vibrato is a handy asset. My picky ear for vibrato has helped many mediocre singers sound astoundingly good during recording sessions. Even though I often have to direct their every move while they're in front of the microphone, they learn from the session and do better the next time!!

Many voice teachers and singers claim that vibrato should develop naturally without training. Some even claim that it can't and shouldn't be taught!! These lines of thinking are dated. I have also found that singers who use exercises to develop their vibrato usually can do it better and with more control than singers who chance upon vibrato development "naturally." I sincerely hope that this chapter will be read by everyone skeptical of vibrato development. I've been teaching singers how to develop vibrato now for eight years. It really does work!!

QUOTES FROM STUDENTS OF THOMAS APPELL

Nancy Scott: *"I knew about vibrato, but I had no idea there were so many different ways to change the quality of it. It took me awhile to be able to recognize what good vibrato sounded like, and when I got to that point, I realized I had a lot of work to do. At first the exercises seemed difficult, and I had a hard time believing that I would ever be able to do the faster speeds well. I felt like quitting many times when I began to realize how much there was to learn about singing that I didn't know and couldn't do. If you have any pride, it can be very intimidating. I am glad I stuck with it because now vibrato is one of the best parts of my vocal technique!!"*

Joe Naab: *"A great golfer is supposed to have a swing that is 'natural', that flows smoothly. You're not supposed to have to think about every detail of the movement...you just do it. But you have to realize how much practice it takes to get to that point. Beginning golfers think about everything until they've hit so many golf balls that it comes naturally. This is exactly how vibrato development works. When I first started training with Thomas to develop my vibrato, I couldn't do it at all. The beginning exercises felt very unnatural, but after a lot of hard work my vibrato developed into an effortless stream that now feels very natural."*

CHAPTER 18
How to Develop Style

A few years ago I was in a nightclub in Newport Beach watching a singer tear his throat apart, straining for the high notes. After his set, I went over and politely told him he needed to take some voice lessens and get some good vocal technique or he wasn't going to have much of a throat left to sing with. I'll never forget his reply. He mentioned one noted voice teacher and said, "A lot of my friends have trained with so-and-so. And, well, I don't know. They may have learned some great vocal technique, but they all end up sounding stupid when they sing!" His friends were all singing Top 40 tunes, but their vocal coach made them use operatic styling and tones for everything they sang... and yes, it probably sounded ridiculous. While this guy didn't have much technique, he had style, and he didn't want to lose his style by learning some wonderful new way to sing that could cost him his job.

After hearing this singer's reply, I walked away saying to myself, "I sure don't want anybody to say something like that about any of my students." At that moment I decided I would find out as much as I possibly could about how to develop style and then devise a way to teach it to my students. The first thing I did was to start really listening to my favorite singers. I wanted to see if I could hear what they were doing that sparked a flame. I found five things that helped make a song stylish.

The Five Ingredients of Song Style

1) The way the artist pronounced the words.

2) The ornamentation (all of the things the singer sang around the melody line, not usually written in the music).

3) The artist's use of vibrato.

4) The vocal tone and intensity.

5) The way the artist used emotion to communicate the message in the song.

How to Develop Style

I found that to really wire a particular style, I had to sing along with the very best singers in that style and learn their tricks. I had to almost become them until their stylish traits started coming out of me naturally.

Guitarists are masters of this art. It works something like this. Picture a young kid about 13 years old who just got his first electric guitar. He puts on a CD and learns every lick in "Eruption" by Eddie Van Halen. Then it's "The Cliffs of Dover" by Eric Johnson, and on and on. Guitarists emulate every nuance of their guitar heroes not to sound like them, but to steal their tricks!! When they start to play, they grab from their bag of tricks. It's like making a withdrawal from the bank. They have to have something in the account if they want to take something out. The best guitarists take these tricks and combine them in new ways that are uniquely their own to create a style.

That is exactly how to develop a vocal style. The best way to become a passionate singer oozing with emotion is to copy, emulate, and mimic other passionate singers who are oozing with emotion!! It rubs off!!

You learn their tricks and then combine them in new ways that are uniquely your own. To get these tricks, you have to sink some roots into the very best singers you can find and draw from them. Learn what makes them tick. Learn what it is about them that you like. Learn to emulate their vocal qualities, not in order to sound like them, but to find and learn vocal maneuvers in their style of music that you may want to use in an original way. When you sing, you don't need to sound exactly like anyone else. The direction you head stylistically will be influenced but not mandated by the singers you've emulated.

It's also important not to listen to bad examples of any style of music. Those rub off, too. You've probably heard the expression, "If you lie down with the dogs, you'll get up with the fleas." This concept is true with singing, too. If you listen to a lot of lame singers, you're going to be influenced by them. You'll find yourself humming their tunes the way they sang it. What you want to do is program your brain with sizzling hot examples of the very best. If that's all you listen to, it will begin to seem very natural for you to sing that way, too. A very famous black saxophone player was once asked how he got his style. His reply: "I don't listen to no bad players." This guy has a good point. Don't let yourself be influenced stylistically by bad examples of anyone singing anything!! Be careful of what your ears hear!! Remember:

The *most effective* way to develop into a stylish singer is to emulate other stylish singers.

I have found that beginning singers without much experience can sound quite stylish when they copy their favorite artist, but they usually sound terrible stylizing anything original... at first. It takes a lot of listening and learning to be so good at singing a style that it just flows out. Experienced singers get to the point where they almost don't have to think about it. They develop a sense of what to do.

I once heard an interview with Jack Russell of the band Great White. He was remembering how, when recording their latest album, he had a hard time sounding fresh on the tunes the band had been playing live because he had sung them so many times they were beginning to sound "rehearsed." His solution was to learn some of the new songs for the album in the studio before he had a chance to remember how to sing them. He figured his improvising would be authentic and spontaneous because he wouldn't really know how he was going to sing each phrase until he got there. Some of the tunes that made it to the album were first takes of songs he learned on the spot in the studio. That's what I call experienced. This guy has style.

If you have developed your style to the point where your singing sounds great without much planning or rehearsal, you're at the top of the ladder. If you're not there yet, you'll get to that point a lot quicker by learning how to emulate and doing a lot of it. Besides emulating vocal ornaments, you also will need to learn how to absorb and impart the emotion like your favorite singers. You can learn to laugh, learn to cry, and learn to feel what you're singing by watching them. Audiences like to see singers bleed on stage. Give them a piece of your heart. Style without emotion is lifeless.

When you feel like you've learned enough by studying other artists to start developing your own style, it's time to start working by yourself. Most of the singers I know who do original material with a unique style spend a lot of time on their own. Once you have a general idea of the direction you want to go, do a lot of performing and recording. Listen to yourself. Listen to what others say about your singing. Find out what works best for your voice and personality. Your style should be effortless. It should be a part of you that's real. Style is sincere. When you sing about how your baby left you, you had darn well better have tears in your eyes. On stage, style can be an attitude. It means going out of your way to have a look, a character, a personality about you. Style communicates emotion. When you sing a song and the audience understands what you're trying to say, that's one thing. But when you sing a song and make the audience feel what you're feeling, that's style. Once you start to define your style, you'll probably have to work at getting it just right. Like trying on shoes, sometimes you have to try on a number of pairs before you find one that fits you just right.

This chapter was written primarily for singers who don't have much style and want to develop it. Some singers have a certain "knack" for being stylish, and I don't want to take away from that. It's valid. Consider yourself fortunate for however much of it you were born with!!

Also, it's important to know that good vocal technique can be applied to any style. When I say "good vocal technique," I am talking about being able to sing any way you want on any note with any vowel or consonant sound. There is no such thing as a universally "correct" way of singing when it comes to style. What's correct for one tune or style might sound ridiculous on another. The "correct" way to sing is a subjective variable entirely dependent upon the good taste of the singer and the teacher of

Can You Sing a HIGH "C"-
Without Straining?

singing. You just wouldn't sing the tenor aria from Handel's "Messiah" the same way Paul McCartney sang "Oh Darlin" from the Beatles' *Abbey Road* album. You just wouldn't!!

Many voice teachers are sadly lacking in good taste when it comes to modern styles of music. They often can't distinguish the tonal qualities associated with classical singing from singing in general. If it doesn't sound operatic, it's not correct.* Consequently, their students end up with a very warped perception of what singing should sound like and are afraid to sing otherwise for fear of not sounding like they were instructed. Only a few years ago, a staff professor lecturing at California State University – Fullerton boldly stated to his class that the "rock" style of music was so "base" and devoid of musical noteworthiness, that it didn't even qualify as an art form and shouldn't even be called music. Could you imagine what you would sound like if this guy were your voice teacher?

There are vocal coaches with good taste who can help contemporary singers develop a vocal technique that will complement their style. If you have got a lot of style but are short on vocal technique, don't be afraid to train your voice. Just take your time and look for a vocal coach who understands your musical point of view.

*Some of the world's greatest singers have chosen to sing in an operatic style. I often admire their vocal technique. However, it would be in bad taste to use operatic styling, (strict pronunciation, extremely low laryngeal positions, vibrato on just about everything, and for the girls, all of the high notes in falsetto) if you were fronting a rock band.

QUOTES FROM STUDENTS OF THOMAS APPELL

Nancy Scott: *"I do all original music, and I never realized how important it is to sing the lyrics of my songs with just the right ornamentation. Before I trained with Thomas, I couldn't really tell when I was stressing a word the wrong way, or using a vibrato quality that sounded funky, or singing with a tone that didn't suit the style of my music. To prepare me for singing my own material, Thomas spent about three months working on my vocal technique. Then he sculpted my style by judiciously choosing artists for me to emulate who were doing the kinds of vocal licks he knew I would need for my songs. I was a little skeptical of how learning someone else's style would help me with my own without compromising my individuality. However, now I can say that I am a lot more creative in my expression and songwriting because I learned so many different runs and licks from all of the copy tunes we worked on. I don't sound like any of the artists I emulated. I use their tricks, but apply them in my own way."*

George Martinovich: *"You get style by copying. I came from Hungary, so when I started singing in American nightclubs, doing top 40 music, I had to learn how to copy the American singers. I got pretty good at sounding like most of the popular artists. People were always surprised to hear me speak because I have a thick accent that doesn't come out in my singing. I also write my own music, and it was by copying the American singers that I found out what I wanted to sound like. I developed a clear picture of my style by combining the attributes I liked from other singers."*

Jim Welty: *"I've trained with Thomas for almost three years now. I knew I had come a long way, but I didn't realize how far until I went back and listened to my first lesson. I could hardly believe the difference!! I feel like no stone has been left unturned as far as the development of my voice is concerned. My sense of style and vocal technique have improved more than I could have ever imagined. I've learned hundreds of vocal licks from singers like Steve Perry, Mickey Thomas, Sam Cook, Brad Delp, Michael Bolton, Bryan Duncan, Amy Grant, John Schlitt, Whitney Houston, and Mariah Carey. Vocal exercises alone are not enough. You have to put as much time and effort into your style development as you do your vocal technique if you want to sound really good."*

CHAPTER 19
The Vocal Production Worksheet

I am kind of lazy at times, especially when it comes to learning new tunes. I used to sit in front of my tape player listening over and over to the songs I wanted to learn. It felt like it took forever to pick out all of the little things the singer was doing, and it was easy to forget the things I had figured out. When teaching, I needed a frame of reference, something I could refer to that would help me convey the tiniest element of style in the tunes, and sheet music just didn't cut it. It was too inaccurate. That's why I developed and now use vocal production worksheets for every song I want to copy. In this chapter I'll explain how you can use vocal production worksheets to capture every ornament in the vocal performance of singers you want to emulate.

A vocal production worksheet is a handwritten outline of a song. The lyrics to the tune are written out phonetically using the International Phonetic Alphabet (IPA) along with notes for ornamentation.

THE INTERNATIONAL PHONETIC ALPHABET

Originally, the IPA was used to help singers sing in foreign languages with perfect pronunciation. Someone who spoke only English could write out a song phonetically and vocalize with flawless German or Italian.

The IPA is also used in missionary work with people who have no written language. Missionaries go into a village and just start pointing at things. The natives tell them what the object is in their own language and the missionaries write down the sounds phonetically using the IPA. After only a few days, the missionaries can begin conversing with near perfect dialect.

Singers who have a conservative singing background, especially those who have done a lot of classical singing, can find that singing R&B, pop, country, or rock is just as foreign as another language. Using the IPA, it is easy to learn the pronunciation in these styles and sound quite convincing. The IPA is a quantum leap above the absurdly limited method of trying to convey sounds by writing "eeeeee," "Ah," etc. To understand how to use the IPA, you will need to purchase *A Pronouncing Dictionary Of*

The Vocal Production Worksheet

American English, published by Merriam-Webster. I know of no better reference book for the IPA.

Before we begin the worksheet, let me say that you don't have to write out the songs you want to copy phonetically using the IPA. It does take some time to learn, and some singers may find learning the IPA too difficult. That's OK. The IPA is the best way to learn subtle pronunciations, but you can still benefit from a vocal production worksheet if you write out the lyrics in English.

To begin your worksheet, write out the song in phrases using the IPA and ending each phrase at a breath point. Some phrases may have just one word and others may be quite long, but stick to one breath per line. When singing, it feels very natural to follow your worksheet in phrases that are one breath long. Phrasing a worksheet by breath points also makes it easy for your eyes to skip down to the next line without interrupting the singing. If you are going to record the song, having the worksheet phrased by breath points makes it easy to track punch-in spots, since punch-ins are always spliced between breaths. You should write out every word of the song in order. If a chorus repeats, write it out again. Even though the words are the same, you may sing it differently the second time and your notation would change.

Always write out the lyrics in light of the ornamentation. If the singer is doing a run on a particular syllable, I'll separate it from the rest of the word with a dash. This makes the worksheet easier to follow. Write neatly. Your worksheets don't have to be a work of art, but if they're sloppy, you'll have a harder time following them, and so will anyone else who has to read them. I always use pencil and 8-1/2" X 11" paper for my worksheets. Never use ink on a worksheet. You may want to change something at a later date.

To help you see how to prepare a vocal production worksheet, I've chosen to prepare a worksheet for a portion of a song I wrote entitled, "A Cure For a Broken Heart." This tune has a lot of great licks that would be tough to remember by rote, making it a perfect candidate for a worksheet.

Can You Sing a HIGH "C"-
Without Straining?

A Cure For a Broken Heart
by Thomas Appell ©1991

maɪ bebi əzə lɛf mi fə sʌmbʌde nu

aɪm laɪ-ən hɪr wʊndɛd ɛn bli-dɛ→ʌn

hi ʃæ-dɪd maɪ hart lɛfd ɪt brɔkɪn ɪntʊ

aɪm filən ðə hɜd ɛ n ðə pe→ɪn

kra-ɪn maɪsɛlf af tə slip ɛvrɪ naɪdə

aɪm filən bətred ɛn mɪstridɛd

maɪ hard əz bɪn brɔkɪn ɪntʊ wan mɔ taɪm

mebi jʊ nɔ haʊ aɪ fi......l →

bət ðɛr ɪz ə kjɔr fɔr ə brɔkɪn hart

ɪt maɪt bi ə mɔmɪnd əwe

wʌn lʊk ɪn ði aɪz əv ə nu faʊ-nd lʌvɜ

kən tek al ðæt hardek ə-we.....ɪ →

ðɛr ɪz ə kjɔr fɔr ə brɔkɪn hart

lʌv ɪz ði ɔnəli we

ðɛr ɪz ə kjɔr fɔr ðə brɔ-kɪn har-dɪd

ʌ kjɜ fɔr ə brɔ-kɪn ha.....rt

90

The Vocal Production Worksheet

You should review the different stages of development for the vocal production worksheet while listening to the vocal performance of "A Cure For a Broken Heart" presented on the cassette tape accompanying this book.

The first step in preparing a worksheet is to write out the lyrics phonetically in phrases separated by breath points (see page 90).

After the lyrics have been written out phonetically, the next step is to note where the artist enunciated a vowel sound and where the vowel sound was run together with the preceding consonant or vowel.

ENUNCIATION

The physical action required to enunciate a vowel is called a "glottal stop." The glottis is the opening between the vocal cords. When you stop your glottis, the cords are closed and air pressure builds up behind them. If you sing a vowel while abruptly opening the cords, it will be enunciated. On your worksheet, enunciated vowels are noted by a vertical tick on the left-hand side of the vowel.

A vowel sound is run together with the preceding consonant or vowel when the glottis is kept open and the flow of air (and the sound) from the cords is uninterrupted while changing from sound to sound. Vowels that are run together with the preceding consonant or vowel are noted with a horizontal dash between the two sounds. Every vowel sound that starts a word is either ticked or dashed. Consonants are usually but not always enunciated. When singing a "T" or "K" at the end of the word, you have the choice of articulating the consonant or "stopping" it. I do not use any notation to denote stopped or unstressed consonants. I place a vertical "tick" on the left-hand side of consonants which are obviously articulated. You'll be surprised by how much you can learn from great singers by just noting how they enunciate (see page 92).

Can You Sing a HIGH "C"- Without Straining?

A Cure For a Broken Heart
by Thomas Appell ©1991

maɪ bebi—əzə lɛf mi fə sʌmbʌde nu

aɪm lâɪ—ən hɪr wʊndɛd—ɛn bli—dɛ→ʌn

hi ʃæ—dɪd maɪ hart lɛfd—ɪt brɔkɪn—ɪntʊ

'aɪm filən ðə hɜd—ɛ—n ðə pe→in

kra—ɪn maɪsɛlf—af tə slip—ɛvrɪ naɪdə

'aɪm filən bətred—ɛn mɪstridɛd

maɪ hard—əz bɪn brɔkɪn—ɪntʊ wʌn mɔ taɪm

mebi jʊ nɔ haʊ—aɪ fi.....l →

bət ðɛr—ɪz—ə kjɔr fɔr—ə brɔkɪn hart

'ɪt maɪt bi—ə mɔmɪnd—əwe

wʌn lʊk—ɪn ði—aɪz—əv—ə nu faʊ—nd lʌvɜ

kən tek—al ðæt hardek—ə—we.....ɪ →

ðɛr—ɪz—ə kjɔr fɔr—ə brɔkɪn hart

lʌv—ɪz ði—ɔnəli we

ðɛr—ɪz—ə kjɔr fɔr ðə brɔ—kɪn har—dɪd

'ʌ kjɜ fɔr—ə brɔ—kɪn ha.....rt

92

The Vocal Production Worksheet

Now that you've written out the lyrics phonetically and noted the enunciated and run-together vowel sounds and consonants, the next step is to write out the ornamentation.

ORNAMENTATION

Ornamentation can be defined as all of the things the artist sings in addition to, or in place of, the melody line. I note two primary ornaments: grace notes and vibrato. I also note miscellaneous ornaments: exhales, cries, yelps, yodels, reverse yodels, vocal fries, and any other unusual sounds made by the singer.

A grace note is any note sung in addition to, or in place of, the melody line. You know what vibrato, exhales and vocal fries are (see chapters 17, 11, and 12, respectively). A cry is a quick pitch drop. A yelp is a quick pitch rise. A yodel is created by going from full voice to falsetto abruptly, making your voice break on purpose. Check out the tunes "Two of a Kind Workin' On a Full House" by Garth Brooks and "Blue" by Leanne Rimes for great displays of yodeling. A reverse yodel is created whenever you go abruptly from falsetto to full voice. For this trick, check out the tune "Because You Loved Me" by Celine Dion. She uses subtle reverse yodels throughout the song.

In our worksheets, I note all pitch changes on every vowel sound using stick-figure musical notation on imaginary staffs. You get to see a visual picture of what the song is doing without having to take the time to transcribe it to music. Your ear gets a great workout by having to really listen to what the artist is doing, and by the time you get to the end of your worksheet, just by doing the worksheet, you will have learned the song!! It's fun to do worksheets on songs you think you "know." You'll be surprised at how much is in the tune that you never realized was there!!

Can You Sing a HIGH "C"- Without Straining?

A Cure For a Broken Heart
by Thomas Appell ©1991

maɪ bebi–əzə lɛf mi fə sʌmbʌde nʊ

aɪm lɒɪ–ən hɪr wʊndɛd–ɛn bli–dɛ→ʌn

hi ʃæ–dɜd maɪ hɑrt lɛfd–ɪt brɔkɪn–ɪntʊ

'aɪm filən ðə hɜd–ɛ–n ðə pe→in

kra–ɪn maɪsɛlf–af tə slip–ɛvrɪ naɪdə

'aɪm filən bətred–ɛn mɪstridɛd

maɪ hɑrd–əz bɪn brɔkɪn–ɪntʊ wʌn mʊ taɪm

mebi jʊ nɔ haʊ–aɪ fi......l →

bət ðɛr–ɪz–ə kjɔr fɔr–ə brɔkɪn hɑrt

'ɪt maɪt bi–ə mɔmɪnd–əwe

wʌn lʊk–ɪn ði–aɪz–əv–ə nʊ faʊ–nd lʌvɜ

kən tek–al ðæt hɑrdek–ə–we.....ɪ →

ðɛr–ɪz–ə kjɔr fɔr–ə brɔkɪn hɑrt

lʌv–ɪz ði–ɔnəli we

ðɛr–ɪz–ə kjɔr fɔr ðə brɔ–kɪn hɑr–dɪd

'ʌ kjɜ fɔr–ə brɔ–kɪn hɑ.....rt

94

The Vocal Production Worksheet

A Cure For a Broken Heart
by Thomas Appell ©1991

maɪ bɛbi—əzə lɛf mi fə sʌmbʌde nu

aɪm lɑɪ-ən hɪr wʊndɛd—ɛn bli-dɛ→ʌn

hi ʃæ-dɜd maɪ hɑrt lɛfd—ɪt brɔkɪn—ɪntʊ

'aɪm filən ðə hɜd— ɛ—n ðə pe→in

kra—ɪn maɪsɛlf—af tə slip—ɛvrɪ naɪdə

'aɪm filən bətred—ɛn mɪstridɛd

maɪ hɑrd—əz bɪn brɔkɪn—ɪntʊ wʌn mɔ taɪm

mebi jʊ nɔ haʊ—aɪ fi.....l →

bət ðɛr—ɪz—ə kjɔr fɔr—ə brɔkɪn hɑrt

'ɪt maɪt bi—ə mɔmɪnd— əwe

wʌn lʊk—ɪn ði—aɪz—əv—ə nu faʊ-nd lʌvɜ

kən tek—al (VF) ðæt (VF) hɑrdek—ə—we.....ɪ →

ðɛr—ɪz—ə kjɔr fɔr—ə brɔkɪn hɑrt

lʌv—ɪz ði—ɔnəli we

ðɛr—ɪz—ə (VF)kjɔr fɔr ðə (VF)brɔ-kɪn (C) hɑr-dɪd

'ʌ kjɜ fɔr—ə brɔ-kɪn hɑ.....rt

95

Can You Sing a HIGH "C"-
Without Straining?

I'll put the grace notes on first and then add the vibrato notation and miscellaneous ornaments on a second sheet so you can see the development of the worksheet step-by-step (see pages 94 and 95).

The last thing to note on the worksheet is the dynamics – the intensity of each note measured by the tension on the vocal cords and the volume.

DYNAMICS

Using a tension scale of 1-10, I write a small number representing the tension under words where the artist sings with a unique or significant intensity. Tensions 1-4 represent varying degrees of falsetto. A tension of 5 would be stronger than falsetto but not quite a full voice. Tensions 6-10 represent varying degrees of full voice.* If there's a lot of air in the tone, I'll note it by the tension with a capital "A" on the right-hand side of the tension number (3A, 4A, etc.). I usually note significant volume changes by a crescendo or decrescendo symbol (see page 97).

When recording or performing with a microphone and especially when using a limiter, the recorded or amplified volume can be kept within certain boundaries no matter how loud you sing. A whisper can be heard at the same volume as a shout, which means that singers these days can add a lot of texture to their songs by singing with loose or tight tensions for soft or strong tones. The vocal production worksheet is a perfect vehicle for learning these dynamic changes.

---

* Refer to page 22 for an explanation of vocal cord tensions and the difference between falsetto and full voice.

The Vocal Production Worksheet

A Cure For a Broken Heart
by Thomas Appell ©1991

maɪ bebi—əzə lɛf mi fə sʌmbʌde nu

aɪm laɪ—ən hɪr wʌndɛd—ɛn bli—dɛ→ʌn

hi ʃæ—dɪd maɪ hart lɛfd—ɪt brɔkɪn—ɪntʊ

'aɪm filən ðə hɜd—ɛ—n ðə pe→ɪn

kra—ɪn maɪsɛlf—af tə slip—ɛvrɪ naɪdə

'aɪm filən bətred—ɛn mɪstrɪdɛd

maɪ hard—əz bɪn brɔkɪn—ɪntʊ wʌn mɔ taɪm

mebi jʊ nɔ haʊ—aɪ fi.,...l →

bət ðɛr—ɪz—ə kjɔr fɔr—ə brɔkɪn hart

'ɪt maɪt bi—ə mɔmɪnd—əwe

wʌn lʊk—ɪn ði—aɪz—əv—ə nu faʊ—nd lʌvɜ

kən tek—al (VF) ðæt (VF) hardek—ə—we,.....ɪ →

ðɛr—ɪz—ə kjɔr fɔr—ə brɔkɪn hart

lʌv—ɪz ði—ɔnəli we

ðɛr—ɪz—ə (VF) kjɔr fɔr ðə (VF) brɔ—kɪn © har—dɪd

'ʌ kjɜ fɔr—ə brɔ—kɪn ha.....rt

97

Can You Sing a HIGH "C"-
Without Straining?

Vocal production worksheets are fast and efficient. With practice, you can learn a song in about an hour. The pronunciation will be perfect, the runs will be easy to see and practice because they're written out, and if you come back a few weeks later to work on a tune, you won't have to worry about forgetting anything. And best of all, the worksheets are always more accurate than sheet music that you buy from the store, but you don't have to know how to read music to follow them!!

If you are in a copy band doing the usual five-night-per-week club scene performing top 40 music, these worksheets will be a godsend to you. They will help you to do a much better job of learning cover material in a fraction of the time it would take to learn it any other way.

Just last week I got a call to help produce a country tune. The artist who wrote the song wanted me to stylize the tune, record myself singing it, and then let him learn the new version by emulating my tricks. I listened to the tune and instantly liked it. I knew I could do the job, but this fellow only gave me five days from the time I first heard the tune to the recording date.

I got right to work on a vocal production worksheet. My vocal runs had to be pretty well-defined because I was planning on many of them to be surrounded by three-part harmony. There was no way I was going to remember by rote all of the licks I was coming up with, so I wrote them out just like I did in "A Cure For a Broken Heart." Country music has a distinct flavor, so I used the International Phonetic Alphabet to write out the lyrics, custom tuning the pronunciation of key phrases. I asked two of my female students who are familiar with vocal production worksheets to sing background harmony for the tune. I prepared vocal production worksheets for their parts too, and threw in some tasty licks written in stick-figure notation. We sounded great together on the recording date and pulled of the session smoothly. The vocal production worksheets played a significant role in helping us record the tune so well in such a short time.

Record producers can make their job a lot easier by using vocal production worksheets as a guide during pre-production when working with a singer.

The Vocal Production Worksheet

Even if the singer is sizzling hot and needs little direction, the worksheets can be a useful aid on and before the recording date. If the singer needs a lot of work, the worksheets become invaluable.

A well-known producer I know of once spent 24 hours recording one three-minute lead vocal line for an artist's demo. The singer landed a major record deal with the demo, but I am sure that the song could have been recorded much faster with the right communication fostered by both producer and artist using vocal production worksheets.

The version of "A Cure For a Broken Heart" that you'll hear on the Vocal Example CD accompanying this book was performed by one of my favorite female singers, Tracy King. On the recording date Tracy and I used vocal production worksheets as a guide. Her worksheet was typewritten in English. I directed her every move from the control room, using a mic wired into her headphones to sing the phrases to her the way I wanted them to come out. My singing examples helped, but I don't think we could have recorded the tune in one session without our worksheets. There was just too much to remember. It was the worksheets that made the difference.

QUOTES FROM STUDENTS OF THOMAS APPELL

Dean Howell: *"When I used to sing songs with the radio, I didn't realize how much of what was really happening in the vocal line I was missing. Thomas taught me how to recognize all of the little things going on in a song that really make it come alive — the grace notes, vibrato, pronunciation, and different kinds of vocal tones. Then he showed me how to write these things down using vocal production worksheets. The worksheets really work!! They force you to listen carefully to the stylistic elements in the songs you sing. I think you learn the licks better when you have to write them out. Sometimes I will listen to a line and say to myself, 'Yeah, I've got that one down,' but when I prepare the worksheet, I usually find some subtle twist to the phrasing that I didn't and probably wouldn't have noticed without notating the ornaments."*

CHAPTER 20
How to Train, Practice, and Warm Up for Singing

HOW TO TRAIN YOUR VOICE

Private vocal instruction is the best way to train a voice. Group instruction doesn't work - at least not very well. If you have several different singers in a group lesson, notes that are easy for one vocalist to sing may be killing the next. What's too fast for some may be too slow and easy for others. Every singer has specific needs and limits and should be given specific, finely tuned exercises to assure safe, effective development.

I like to give my students 1-2 one-hour sessions of private instruction each week. For the first twelve hours we spend the entire hour working on vocal technique. I could start working with a student on a song after the first couple of lessons, but it's really not in their best interest. They wouldn't have developed enough skill in their throat to follow the direction I would be giving them on how to sing the tune. After the twelfth lesson, they're usually ready for song work and I split the workouts to one hour of technique and a one hour of song work each week.

Hour technique lessons work better than half hour technique lessons, and training more often works better than training less often. I have a little saying, "Never sing a note in full voice that you haven't sung in falsetto first." If you follow this advice you will be giving your voice a proper warm-up sequence. I *always* do falsetto work and exercises to smooth out break points between registers before any exercises that really work a student's full voice in a lesson. This takes about 30 minutes. These exercises are generally not strenuous. The rest of the lesson is spent on exercises that *are* strenuous... like extending the range of a student's full voice and developing stamina. To do these exercises correctly takes a solid half an hour. Do the math. A one hour technique lesson is the way to go.

Many students want to advance at a faster pace and train with me two hours per day separated by a 3-4 hour break. This works especially well if I can see them 5-6 days in a row. That much supervised training develops an extremely solid understanding of vocal technique that is often more complete than students training at lesser intervals.

WORKING ON SONGS

The best way to learn how to sing songs well and become a really stylish singer is to emulate other really stylish singers. I can't over-emphasize this point. Even if you do original music, it's still good to learn tricks and vocal runs from whoever's hot and current. Musical styles are constantly changing, and it's good to always be trying new things with your voice to continue to expand your potential. The best way to learn these new things is to emulate.

Sing along with your favorite CDs, The more the better. Try your best to emulate every single thing the singer does. If you have the time, always make a vocal production worksheet and follow it while practicing. If you *don't* make vocal production worksheets, you are sure to miss out on some cool tricks in the tunes you sing. As soon as possible, start buying or making accompaniment tracks of the tunes you sing and practice singing with musical accompaniment only.

Record yourself singing. If you think you're sounding hot and you really want to know, this is the way to find out. A recording is the ultimate test for determining whether you're as slick as you think you are.

TRAINING CHILDREN

It's OK to start training children as early as they can handle the discipline of a lesson. Don't think that just because a child is young he or she should not be allowed to have good voice training. How do you think singers like Leanne Rimes, Britney Spears, Brandy, and many others became superstars in their teens? They started taking their singing seriously when they were very young. Kids need the same technique and song work that adults need, and if you can get your child to be disciplined and practice, you might have a potential superstar on your hands in a few years.

Can You Sing a HIGH "C"-
Without Straining?

Learning to master all of the things I've written about in this book... extending the range of your full voice, developing great sounding vibrato, and learning to control the tone of your voice to name a few, is difficult to do on your own. Particularly with the full voice exercises, the subtle differences in tonality that guide you towards adduction are tough to distinguish from an increased pull. Most singers need time with a good vocal instructor to really maximize their potential. Get private vocal instruction from a good teacher. There's no better way to improve your voice.

HOW TO PRACTICE

You should plan on practicing vocal technique exercises one hour per day 5-6 days per week. I often train singers who take two one-hour lessons per day, once in the early afternoon and once in the evening, with great results. After your technique fundamentals are in good shape, try two hours in a row, the first hour warming up and working out with vocal exercises and the second hour devoted to song work and style development. I wouldn't recommend much more than two hours of vocalizing per day, even if you have the extra time.

Individual voices do vary, and some singers can handle more work while others will need to do less to keep their vocal cords in healthy shape. You might start an hour of technique per day and see how you feel. If it's no problem try the two-hour-split-workout mentioned above. Don't sing to the point where you begin experiencing hoarseness. A little dryness, OK, but no hoarseness. You'll run the risk of damaging your vocal cords.

Also, the amount of speaking you do will have a lot to do with how much singing you can do safely on any given day. You probably wouldn't be able to practice two hours on a day where you spoke for two hours. Even using good vocal technique, there's just so much mileage you can put on a healthy set of cords each day until they become overworked. Technique practice on your own is best accomplished by singing along with a recording of a private voice lesson.

How to Train, Practice, and Warm Up for Singing

Overworking your voice can cause vocal nodules. Underworking your voice slows down the improvement process. If you are doing a vocal workout, when you finish you should feel worked out. Fatigue associated with hard work builds strength. Think of it like going to the gym. If you want to build up the vocal cords, which are muscles, you've got to work them hard. Arnold Schwarzenegger did not build the muscles in his incredible physique by stopping his workout as soon as it began to feel difficult. Don't think that you're going to develop a powerful voice and an amazing range by doing easy workouts.

For example, the exercises for extending the range of your full voice can be quite strenuous. At times you could even say it hurts. After finishing a workout if you feel the kind of discomfort associated with working a muscle within safe limits, like when bench pressing or doing squats, you're probably doing the exercise correctly. The kind of discomfort you feel from working a muscle the right way is really just acute fatigue. The sharp pain you get from overworking or injuring a muscle is much different from the normal discomfort you might expect from a tough workout and you need to be able to tell the difference.

Take one day off each week and rest your voice - 24 hours in a row with no singing. This means no singing to your vocal workout CDs, no singing in the shower, no singing period. Make your day off the same day each week. Your voice likes to be worked out routinely and it likes to rest routinely. If you practice and/or perform seven days a week, your voice will not progress as quickly as if you sang for six days. Singers who sing seven days a week can count on experiencing vocal problems directly related to not giving their voice a proper rest. You need one day off from singing each week mentally and physically. Take it.

Whatever you're worst at practice the most. If you have a particular vowel or consonant that plays havoc on your vocal technique, practice it every day until it's mastered. If you practice whatever you're worst at every day, pretty soon that will be one of your best sounds. Then you should pick a new worst sound and practice that every day.

WARMING UP YOUR VOICE

Whenever you sing, you should do a vocal warm-up. A warm-up is done for two reasons. First, you need to stretch the cords, limber them up, loosen them up. Athletes who run track always stretch their legs before running a race. When I ran track in high school, the coach always had us stretch our legs and jog a few laps before we did any serious running. After stretching and a warm-up, my stride was significantly increased and I felt a lot more relaxed. After you warm up your voice, high notes should come more easily and singing throughout your entire range should feel more responsive. Remember, a good rule of thumb is to **never sing a note in full voice that you haven't first sung in falsetto**. There's no better preparation for singing high notes strongly than to sing them softly first.

The second reason to do some warm-up exercises is to blow off phlegm that may have been deposited on the cords and might cause your tone to sound froggy. I often have phlegm on my cords when I wake up in the morning, so if I have to sing early, I try to take at least a half hour to warm up. Most singers sound best about 4 hours after awakening. If you have to sing early in the morning, get up early enough to have 4 hours of awake time before you have to sing.

I usually sound best in the early afternoon after a good solid workout, before I've done too much talking. But there are some days my voice feels great five minutes into a vocal workout, or late at night after a long day teaching and speaking. You can't second-guess what your voice is going to feel like when you wake up in the morning. You have to give it what it needs on a day by day basis, adjusting the warm-up time and exercises by how you feel that day. You'll have to find out what's right for you, and you'll find out by trial and error. Just experiment. Too much warm-up might detract from your performance. Not enough and you won't perform as well.

How to Train, Practice, and Warm Up for Singing

For singers with five-night-per-week club work, a two-hour singing limit can still be accomplished if the singing is not going to be continuous for the entire set. On a day when you have to sing for a long time, you would still want to do a vocal warm-up, but make it as short as possible. No matter how long you're singing each day, if you start noticing hoarseness developing as a result of overtraining, cut down on either the amount or intensity of your singing.

Let's review some of the important points in this chapter:

1. Private voice instruction from a good teacher is the best way to train your voice.

2. Start kids with private vocal training as soon as they can handle the discipline of a lesson.

3. The best way to learn how to sing songs well and become a really stylish singer is to emulate other really stylish singers.

4. You should practice vocal technique exercises at least one hour per day.

5. You should practice singing songs one hour per day.

6. Don't practice more than two hours per day.

7. Take one day off each week and rest your voice completely. - 24 hours in a row with no singing.

8. Whatever you're worst at, practice the most.

9. Never sing a note in full voice that you haven't sung first in falsetto.

Can You Sing a HIGH "C"-
Without Straining?

QUOTES FROM STUDENTS OF THOMAS APPELL

Dawn Bullock: *"An important part of my training has been the song work. Developing a great vocal technique is wonderful, but it's not enough. You've got to be able to sing!! Thomas is so skillful at feeding me just the right tunes to put just the right flavor into my style. There are things I've learned about how to be stylish and sincere that I had never thought of before, things like cries, vocal fries, and exhales. I can see now why one-on-one private lessons are the only way to go. I would never have been able to get so much emotion into my singing on my own. It really makes a difference to have my own personal trainer. I used to sing a lot for fun and it sounded OK, but I knew that I could sound better. When I sing now, people stop and listen!!"*

Tim Scott: *"Professional athletes know the importance of proper training before competition. Many hours are spent under the guidance of a good coach honing all of the finer nuances necessary to compete with the best. You would hardly expect a pro basketball or football team to think they could make it on their own without a coach. Athletes know they will perform better under the direction of a personal coach who has worked with them regularly, who knows their strengths and weaknesses, and who can give them helpful direction when they are too closely involved to be objective. Singing is an athletic feat, and singers need the same kind of personal attention as a professional athlete. I wish I would have figured this out sooner. I used to think that because I was a really good musician, my singing should just sort of fall in place by itself. I had pretty well mastered my guitar and keyboard playing, but those were 'instruments' that I had become proficient at through practice. Singing should just happen naturally, right? Nothing could be further from the truth! Six months of vocal training with Thomas has taught me more than six years of vocalizing in showcase bands. While I still have quite a bit to learn, I feel that I am now developing the kind of vocal technique necessary to perform in the higher ranges that I had always struggled with before taking private lessons."*

Can You Sing a HIGH "C"– Without Straining?

PART 3

General Tips for Singing

CHAPTER 21
The Importance of Singing In Tune

I do a lot or recording and producing of vocal lines in the studio. Occasionally I'll get to work with a singer who can sing in tune, but it's rare. Nine out of ten vocal re-takes are related to pitch problems. The style might be there, the emotion happening, but if something is obviously flat or sharp you're not going to keep the take. The same holds true for live performing. No matter how much style or emotion you deliver, if you can't sing in tune, no one will want to listen to you. In this chapter I'll explain why singers tend to sing out of tune and what can be done to improve intonation.

There are only two reasons why you sing out of tune. Either you can't tell where the pitch is supposed to be, or you know exactly where the note is but can't quite make the cords produce it.

There are singers who have a nearly impossible time singing in tune because of a mental block when it comes to identifying pitch. If you are legitimately tone-deaf, you can improve your intonation by doing ear-training exercises with a piano guide under the direction of a vocal coach. You will need a trainer because initially you won't be able to tell whether or not you're singing in tune. Your vocal coach will tell you when you're pitch is on target. After a few weeks of one-on-one coaching you will find yourself developing the ability to recognize what it feels and sounds like to match the pitch on the piano.

I once trained a local dermatologist who could not sing three notes in a row without going way out of tune. He could not even hit the note I would give him when I played it six or seven times in a row for him on the piano. That's what I call a pitch problem. However, he was determined to learn how to sing. After a little over a year of training he developed into a remarkably good singer. His specialty was doing Roy Orbison cover tunes, and to this day I've never heard anyone sing Orbison better.

The Importance of Singing In Tune

It may take many months of training to get to the point where you can correctly sing any pitch you hear. How proficient you become at singing in tune will be directly related to how much time you spend practicing the ear-training exercises.

When you get to the point where you can tell whether or not you're singing in tune, the next step is training the cords to match the pitch of the notes you want to sing. You will be able to sing with perfect intonation initially when going very slowly from note to note. As the speed of the song or exercise you're singing is increased you will have to train the cords not to over or under-shoot the correct pitch.

There are three excellent training methods for improving your intonation after you can accurately perceive pitch.

1. Practice singing scales and arpeggios as fast as you can without going out of tune. Use a metronome to keep track of your speeds and advance when you've mastered a particular speed.

2. Learn all of the musical intervals. A musical interval is simply the distance between two notes. If you have memorized all of the pitch changes you will ever have to make, singing in tune is a lot easier. The best way to learn an interval is to find a familiar song that has the interval in it. For example, to learn a minor third, you might pick the christmas carol Jingle Bells. When you sing "Jingle bells, jingle bells, jin-gle all the way," the "jin" is the root, and the "gle" is the minor third above the root.

3. Record yourself. No hiding here. If you're singing in or out of tune it should be painfully apparent. It's best to record with a producer or vocal coach who will listen critically to each take and help you to evaluate where you were on or off the pitch.

109

Can You Sing a HIGH "C"- Without Straining?

Most singers work to develop a good sense of **relative pitch.** Once you give them a starting note, they can stay in tune. Singers with **perfect pitch** can tell exactly what note they're singing with or without a cue from another instrument. Having perfect pitch is a lot like seeing in color. It's easy for us to distinguish red from orange because they look different. Singers with perfect pitch have the same perception about musical notes. In the same way that red looks quite different than orange, to a singer with perfect pitch an "F" would sound quite different than an "E." They simply have the ability to hear the difference.

You can develop perfect pitch by listening acutely to each note you want to memorize, looking for the subtle differences in tonality that make one note sound different than another. It takes a long time to get perfect pitch if you weren't born with the ability, but if you can develop it by training you'll have a much easier time singing in tune. People with perfect pitch can seem almost spooky. I had a female student who told me she had been born with perfect pitch. She claimed she could tell the pitch of any note just by hearing it. I have to admit, I was a little skeptical, so I decided to put her to the test. I started playing random notes across the entire range of my piano. To my amazement she correctly identified every single note.

Often when you're performing with a band, it's very difficult to hear whether or not you're in tune. A good trick is to try performing live while wearing ear-plugs. The right ear-plug can filter out specific frequencies and allow you to hear the music quite well while your own vocalizing becomes predominant. Custom-fitted wireless in-ear monitors work very well for helping you to stay in tune while singing live. It's like singing with headphones. You get ear protection and monitoring from the same device. A new method to stay in tune during live gigs is with a pitch correcting signal processor that automatically corrects the pitch of every note you sing. Properly adjusted, it kicks in transparently and pulls your singing to the nearest half-step. This little wonder-box works amazingly well. Many famous artists these days won't go on stage without it. The funny part is, the company that makes them is having a hard time getting celebrity endorsements because nobody will admit to using it.

110

QUOTES FROM STUDENTS OF THOMAS APPELL

Tom Kessler: *"The importance of singing in tune cannot be stressed enough. My vocal technique has come a long ways. I can sing in full voice up to 'G' above tenor high 'C' with pretty good tone but I can't start performing yet because my pitch perception is not good enough. It's way better than it was before I started training, but it's got to be near-perfect before an audience will want to hear me."*

Kathy Breen: *"It's expensive to sing out of tune if you happen to have made being a recording artist your chosen profession. If a noticeable part of your singing is out of tune you have to stay there in the studio and keep plugging away until you get it right. This means more studio time for recording and a longer wait for your project to be completed. You can't start generating income from CD sales until you're finished with the recording, and you're not finished with the recording until it's sung in tune. Take my advice. Learn to sing in tune. You'll never regret having perfect intonation."*

CHAPTER 22
Understanding Your Speaking Voice

Many of the singers I've trained who have experienced serious vocal problems got their voices in hot water by speaking incorrectly. In this chapter I'll explain how you can learn to speak safely and comfortably and how you can avoid vocal problems associated with poor speaking habits.

To preserve your vocal cords during speech, there are three very simple rules to follow. First, **never speak on the same pitch for any length of time.** You need to adduct the cords throughout as much of their length as you can while speaking without sounding corny. This will mean adding higher tones to your speech pattern and specifically using chest and head voice while speaking. Most people who get hoarse from speaking, speak in a limited pitch range and wear out that part of the cords due to overuse. Like a guitarist who only plays on one fret, pretty soon that fret will show signs of wear while the others will be fine.

A lot of singers and public speakers are referred to voice pathologists (V.P.) when they start having problems with nodules or chronic hoarseness. One of the first things the V.P. does is try to find what they call the "optimum pitch" of the patient's speaking voice. The patient is then counseled to try to speak at their optimum pitch so as to alleviate the strain which caused their voice to wear out. In actuality, the patient is just going to start speaking with the cords adducted to a different spot, one that isn't irritated yet. If they concentrate their speech at that one point, before too long it will be just as damaged as the part of the cords that caused the problem in the first place. Remember, the solution for preventing a tired, worn-out voice is to never speak on the same pitch for any length of time.

It takes a little practice to get the hang of speaking with a wide range, but it really is effective in eliminating hoarseness. The sales trainer for a large corporation in Orange County came to me after experiencing chronic hoarseness each day after work. "Work" consisted of lecturing new recruits for six to eight hours per day. It took several months of singing exercises for me to teach him how to adduct his vocal cords to be able to create head voice in his speech pattern. Then we spent a few more months working on his delivery. I had him go through the training manual he used at work, page by page, speaking in a monotone at different pitches with perfect vocal technique. It sounded like some sort of Jewish chant, but it sure worked. He doesn't get hoarse anymore, and later he told me that now his recruits say he now sounds a lot more interesting and commanding while teaching because of the wide range of vocal inflections he is able to utilize with his new voice.

The second rule is to **never speak louder than is perfectly comfortable.** This means that you don't talk over loud music, screaming kids, shouting fans, etc. for long periods of time.

A friend of mine was getting married several years ago. The reception was incredible: great food, lots of friends, great music – great, *loud* music. I really knew better, but I was having such a good time, I more or less talked myself into talking over the music for about two hours. I was hoarse the next day, and the next, and the next. I could feel the effect of that reception a month later!! It wasn't worth it!!

If you're at a dance or concert, dance your socks off, but try to resist the temptation to talk over the music. You'll be glad you did.

The third rule is to **stop speaking when you start getting hoarse.** If you continue to abuse your voice after it's warned you by breaking up that it is not feeling well, you are only asking for trouble.

Several years ago I began training a young female singer. She had a nice voice, but there was an obvious break between chest and head voice and her upper end was lacking in power. After about nine months of training, her break point was practically eliminated, her upper end was starting to focus, and her style was beginning to develop. Things were going well.

Then a funny thing happened. Her voice started getting hoarse. I always work my students hard in a lesson, but never to the point where they strain. I knew that she wasn't doing anything in the lesson to damage her voice. After quizzing her, I felt that she was practicing correctly at home too. I asked if she did a lot of talking over loud music or raising her voice. As it turned out, she had just had a baby a few months before she began training. She already had a couple of older kids, and unfortunately for her voice, she was having to shout at her three kids to command their attention. I could see the direction her throat was headed and advised her to stop talking loudly to her children. It was a hard habit to break. After six more months of abusing her speaking voice, she eventually got nodules and her singing was shot. She finally took my advice and went for two weeks without raising her voice once to her kids. Our next voice lesson was the best one in over a year. She couldn't believe what the time off had done for her vocal cords.

Take care of your voice when you speak. You only have one set of vocal cords. Treat them right and they will serve you faithfully for many years. Remember the three keys to a healthy speaking voice: never speak on the same pitch for any length of time, never speak louder than is perfectly comfortable, and stop speaking when you start getting hoarse.

QUOTES FROM STUDENTS OF THOMAS APPELL

Cathy Smith: *"Several years ago when I was leading worship in a small church group, I began experiencing difficulty while singing. There seemed to be a range of notes that was becoming harder and harder to sing through. I struggled along for a few years, but the condition got worse. I finally decided to make an appointment with an ear, nose, and throat doctor. The doctor's diagnosis came as a shock. I had nodules on my vocal cords!! I could either have them surgically removed or go to a speech therapist. The idea of surgery didn't sound too appealing, so I decided to go see a speech therapist.*

The therapist tried to find what she called the 'optimum pitch' of my voice and get me to speak there. Although I didn't know it at the time, speaking continuously at any pitch can be damaging to the cords. It wears them out!! The secret to a healthy speaking voice is to never speak on the same pitch for any length of time. It's better to use as much of the range of your voice while speaking as you can and to train with someone who can teach you how to hit the higher pitches correctly without straining. I was to learn all of this later from Thomas Appell. After eight months of treatment with the speech therapist, I was released. The therapist told me she had helped me as much as she could. Unfortunately, there was no improvement. In fact, the condition had gotten worse. My singing range eventually became so limited that I was forced to quit leading the worship service. My speaking felt uncomfortable. I mentioned this dilemma to a musician friend of mine and he suggested that I make an appointment with Thomas Appell at Vocal Dynamics. I was quite apprehensive. The speech therapist didn't help. What could a singing teacher do?

I've trained with Thomas for about one year now and have noticed significant improvement. The range that I had lost is almost completely restored, and I am seeing new improvement weekly. I am so thankful that I didn't have to undergo surgery. Had I not found Thomas, surgery would have been my next and only alternative. I am hoping to resume my position as worship leader soon. I know that when I do, not only will the problem area of my voice be corrected, but I'll be singing better than I did before I ever had a problem – and with more confidence!!"

115

CHAPTER 23
What to Eat and Drink Before Singing

Students often ask me to recommend something for them to drink that will make their throats feel better prior to a performance. In this chapter, I'll present the best recipe I've found for a vocal potion along with some do's and don'ts for eating and drinking prior to singing.

DRINKING WATER

An often overlooked natural aid to singing is water. You need to become a water-aholic. I recently trained a male singer who sings in a classic rock cover band. He was doing a lot of background singing and a few leads, and had been experiencing severe hoarseness after the second or third song he had to sing in almost every performance. He picked up 5 notes of full-voice range extension after a few lessons, but the hoarseness continued. He swore to me he was really careful with his voice, not talking between sets over the house music, doing his vocal warm-ups before every gig, and generally being vocally conciencious. Then I asked him about how much water he drank. "Water?" was his reply. "I didn't know that it mattered how much water you drink." I suggested he start drinking at least 32 ounces of water per day and see if that made a difference with his singing.

At the next lesson he walked in beaming with this big smile. I knew we had found the answer. He said for the first time *ever*, he was able to sing a whole set with no hoarseness whatsoever. He couldn't believe what a difference drinking water had made to his singing.

One thing to keep in mind when you drink water. If you want to sound great on Friday night, you had better drink a lot of water on Thursday. It seems to take a day or so to get the water into your system so those saliva glands have something to secrete. My advice... get into the habit of regularly drinking a lot of water *every* day. I keep a bottle of water nearby whenever possible and try to drink a little here and there throughout the day.

What to Eat and Drink Before Singing

A SPECIAL POTION

For most singers, drinking lots of water solves the dryness issue. Outside of drinking water, you should try not to depend upon anything but a vocal warm-up and good technique to get you through a performance. But for those times when your throat is really feeling dry and you want some quick temporary relief, mix about 6-8 ounces of water, one fresh squeezed lemon, and 2-3 tablespoons of honey into a nice gooey liquid and gargle. The honey coats the cords, the lemon juice makes you salivate, and the water dilutes the mixture to a potency that is easier to gargle with. I call this little concoction "Liquid Range Extension." It's that good. This stuff really works. If you've got a naturally dry metabolism, this mixture is a godsend. You might try keeping a container of it nearby when you perform so you can reapply as needed.

ASPIRIN

An effective helper for singers with laryngitis is aspirin. When you have laryngitis, the vocal cords are swollen and inflamed, and they don't adduct well at all. It's not uncommon for singers with laryngitis to lose their upper range completely. Aspirin is an anti-inflammatory drug. It causes the swelling to come down. If your upper range has disappeared due to swollen cords, you will be amazed at how effective a little aspirin is in getting those missing notes back. I found out about the value of aspirin from one of my students, a pharmacist who is determined to become the next great opera star. I had a case of laryngitis due to a flu bug that really flared up during a lesson with her, and I couldn't sing a note in head voice. She told me about the aspirin trick and in less than 15 minutes after I downed two aspirin, my entire upper range had come back!!

CHEWING GUM

A lot of singers chew gum while they perform. The gum chewing makes the saliva glands secrete and helps keep the cords nice and moist.

EATING BEFORE YOU SING

If you are going to eat, eat lightly. Abdominal breathing hurts on a full stomach. You can still sing. It just feels really uncomfortable. Don't eat anything really cold. The muscles you use when singing work better when they're warm. Milky things generally gum up your cords. Watery things (like tea) lubricate them. If I eat a bowl of ice cream and then try to vocalize, it sometimes takes a half hour before I can sing up to par. The cold freezes up my cords and the milk gums them. I can't eat any kind of nut or potato chip prior to singing. Foods like these break up on my cords in little pieces and I spend the next half hour choking each time the air passing through my cords blows off a chip.

What to Eat and Drink Before Singing

QUOTES FROM STUDENTS OF THOMAS APPELL

Rich Compeau: *"I started using the water/honey/lemon mixture soon after I began training, and I will have to say that it really helps. I sing a lot of very high energy songs with extremely high notes in full voice and this vocal potion makes my singing feel very smooth in a range that would normally make my voice feel dry. It's great stuff."*

CHAPTER 24
Why Contemporary Singers Shouldn't Go to College

Singers across the nation are crying out to our school system for high-caliber vocal instruction courses emphasizing contemporary music styles. They don't want to learn classical arias. They don't want to spend years studying Italian opera. They do want to learn how to sing the music they hear on the radio and make a living performing it. In this chapter I'll explain some of the reasons why contemporary singers would be better off training with a private vocal instructor than going to college to prepare for a career in singing.

Colleges and universities offer contemporary singing courses, but they're usually geared towards beginning singers. If a vocalist wants to graduate as a vocal performance major in rock, pop, country, or jazz, train intensely, give recitals, get state-funded lessons, etc., there's really no place to go, at least not in the public school system. Some colleges have jazz choirs and pop ensembles, but you can't major in a modern style... at least not yet.

Singers who don't know any better often go through years of training at a university thinking that somehow learning classical opera will prepare them for a career in pop music. It won't. If a singer has been trained to sing in classical and operatic styles, that's what they're going to be good at. This is especially true for female singers. Remember, in classical and operatic styles of singing, all of the girls sing all of the high notes in falsetto. They're not allowed to use full voice when singing and if the subject is even presented, they're usually taught to think that singing in full voice is distasteful. I've trained countless classically-trained female singers who couldn't sing a note in full voice - after many years of voice lessons. Classically trained male singers use full voice, but the pronunciation and tones used are very different from what would be appropriate for pop tunes.

I once trained a female singer who had graduated from USC with a master's degree in vocal performance who had never – get this – never sung in her lower register! She had never sung in full voice and didn't have the foggiest idea what it was or what it was supposed to sound like. She had developed a huge break between her upper and lower registers and had been taught by her teachers at USC to sing everything in reinforced falsetto. Because of this, her low notes were powerless. Imagine trying to sing an "E" below middle "C" in falsetto. When I told her the truth about her vocal technique, she didn't believe me, at least not until her chest voice started coming in. Even then I had to fight tooth-and-nail to get her to accept the fact that she wasn't the vocal virtuoso she liked to think she was. I felt like she blamed me for every weakness I uncovered in her vocal technique. It was tough going, but well worth it.

I'll never forget one of my last lessons with her. Having trained with me for over a year she was getting quite good at controlling the tension of her cords and singing low and high notes with a full voice for the first time. We had just finished working on a song, and as I looked over to tell her what a good job she had done, I noticed she was crying. I was concerned and asked what was the matter. She told me through her tears that she had never dreamed it possible that she would ever be able to sing as beautifully as she had just sung. She thanked me for sticking with her, even when I knew she didn't believe in me. It's moments like those that make me feel so grateful to be able to teach singing.

Even if you want to pursue opera, unfortunately, the universities stress repertoire, not vocal technique. If you go in to college with a great voice you might do OK, but if you go to college with an average voice there's a good chance that you'll come out knowing lots of songs with still an average voice. I would recommend a good college *and* a good private vocal coach if you're considering a classical or operatic career.

At present, the best place to get training for contemporary singing is with a private vocal coach. Your own personal voice trainer will develop your voice to its fullest extent and point your vocal development to a direction geared towards whatever style you want to pursue. You will be on a direct course towards your goal of becoming a singer. If you want some textbook knowledge of music, you can always take music theory classes at a junior college for a very nominal amount of money. But if you want to make a living with your voice, dedicate yourself to the best vocal instructor you can find and get out there and start performing!

Can You Sing a HIGH "C"-
Without Straining?

Don't get me wrong. I support our school system, but the vocal technique taught in most public schools could stand for much improvement. It's about time the music department heads of our universities develop strong strong contemporary music and vocal technique programs in light of the fact that the majority of singers want to study contemporary music and need a voice that will allow them to perform it.

I don't want to give the impression that contemporary styles of singing (rock, pop, etc.) are better than opera or musical theatre. I like opera and musical theatre. The fact is that the general public would rather be singing Top 10 hits. I might get one call a month from someone wanting to actively pursue singing opera or musical theatre and fifty calls from singers wanting to learn how to sing like the singers they hear on the radio. The people who shape the music policy in our school system should realize this trend and do something about it.

Another real problem with singers who plan on going through four years of college is age. The record industry is a youth-oriented business. In the pop-rock genre, a talented 16 year-old with a cool look will have a much better chance of landing a recording contract than a 36 year old. I know producers that won't even consider launching a new artist over the age of 20. Start training early. Go to college. But if you're intent on pursuing a career in popular music, you don't have time to wait until you've graduated from college to start your career. You should be submitting demos to record labels as early as your maturity level and talent allow. If you *are* a little older, don't throw in the towel. Michael Bolton began his career when he was nearly 40 years old. Tina Turner is still rockin' in her fifties. The point is, it's *easier* to get a career started if you start early.

Many years ago, after suffering some physical problems with his legs, a young man was told he would never walk again - at least not very well. A life with canes and crutches was the predicted reality. But this young man didn't believe the doctors. Something inside of him said..."I'm not just going to walk again, I'm going to show everybody that my legs work just fine. I'm going to run." So he started therapy. At first with difficulty, he began walking, then jogging, and before too long, after months of hard work and training, he began to run.

Why Contemporary Singers Shouldn't Go to College

The will to prove that his legs were not just functional, but completely capable drove Roger Bannister to begin competing. His specialty was running the one mile race. At the time it was commonly believed that it was physically impossible for anyone to run a mile in less than four minutes. It had never been done before, and experts believed it would take a miracle for anyone to run that fast. Roger Bannister believed in miracles. An interesting thing happened. The year *after* he became the very first man in history to run a mile in less than four minutes, a number of other runners did the same. All of those runners had the potential to run a mile in less than four minutes all along. It wasn't until they *believed* it could be done that they were able to do it. As long as they thought it was impossible to run a mile in less than four minutes, for them it *was* impossible... until they knew beyond a shadow of doubt that it could be done.

The purpose of this book is to get you to believe, to know that you can sing high notes without straining, develop vibrato, tone control, and become a stylish singer... if you don't mind working for it. Once you see that many, many other singers who had seemingly poor voices before training are now able to sing better than they could have imagined, it is my hope that you will come to know beyond a shadow of doubt that you can improve your voice too.

QUOTES FROM STUDENTS OF THOMAS APPELL

Sandra Chung: *"I took a voice lesson at a local college and stopped going after three weeks. I felt like it was a waste of time for me. There were so many people in the class that no one got significant individual attention, and the few times that we did get one-on-one training from the instructor it was too brief to be really useful. From what I've heard this is pretty typical of college voice classes. They can be fun if you're not that serious about developing your voice, but if you want to really improve your vocal technique you need to take private lessons."*

PRIVATE VOCAL INSTRUCTION

Many of you reading this book will want to develop your voice to it's maximum potential... take it all the way. In order to do that you're going to need private voice lessons.

If you'd like to train with me personally, time permitting, I'll be happy to help. Our first lesson will be approximately 45 minutes long. We'll go over a lot of important fundamentals and I'll get to know exactly what you can and can't do with your voice. After that first session, it takes about 12 hours of instruction to get your voice trained to the point where you can begin working with me on songs and have developed enough skill to follow my direction.

Now, here's some good news. It doesn't have to take 12 weeks to take 12 hours of instruction. Hour lessons work better than half hour lessons, so unless I'm training a child under the age of eight, I always give hour technique lessons. Most students do 1-2 hour lessons per week, but if you'd like to improve at a faster pace, I've had excellent results with singers coming as often as 2 hours per day. This works especially well if you have to fly in from another country to train and can only stay here for a week or two. After the first 12 hours of vocal technique lessons we start working on applying what you've learned to the songs that you bring to me to work with.

The average full-voice range increase for male and female singers training with me is 7 notes. Many singers get 12-15 notes of full-voice range increase, often after the first couple of lessons. We'll also focus on developing vibrato, tone control, breath control, vocal agility, smoothing out break points between registers, and developing style. The goal is to end up with a well-trained voice that sounds great in whatever style of music you like to perform.

I also produce and record music for many of the singers I train. If you'd like to hear some examples of music I've produced, just check out the VDP Publishing website **www.vocalinstruction.com**. The music videos on the website are really cool. My specialty is coaching the singers I record to deliver stunning, heartfelt vocal performances exquisitely recorded using state-of-the-art recording equipment and the most up-to-date computer-based editing technology. The Vocal Dynamics studio phone number is 949.251.1162.

The HIGH "C"
VIDEO TRAINING SERIES
for Male, Female, and Children Singers

This long-awaited video training series is one of the most powerful learning tools ever developed for singers. Each of the three video training series include 12 hours of one-on-one instruction. You'll learn solid fundamentals of good vocal technique by watching and singing along with example singers going through this incredibly effective program. Studying with the HIGH 'C' VIDEO TRAINING SERIES is an absolute must for anyone serious about training their voice! Even if you are taking or plan on taking private lessons, the video series is still a fabulous help in developing your understanding of singing. The easiest way to order your video training series is online at the VDP Publishing website:

www.vocalinstruction.com

If you wish to order by mail, send $399.00 plus $12.00 S/H for each 12 hour series (Please check the VDP Publishing website for current availability). Mail check or money order to:

VDP Publishing
17870 Skypark Circle, Suite 107
Irvine, CA 92614

ABOUT THE AUTHOR

Thomas Appell is a graduate of California State Polytechnic University, Pomona, CA. He graduated in 1979 with a major in engineering and a minor in music. He now lives in Coto de Caza, California with his wife Dianna. His interests include surfing, skiing, and writing music.

Thomas has written two feature articles for MIX magazine - "How To Produce a Vocal Line" and "Producing a Vocal Line." He has written for GIG magazine and was a monthly columnist in CCM Publications Musicline Magazine "Vocal Spotlight" column. He has also served as the junior high Sunday School teacher at Christian Mission Church in Mission Viejo, CA.

Thomas has been training singers full-time since 1982 and specializes in recording, arranging, and producing vocal lines in his state-of-the-art computer-based digital production studio located in Coto de Caza, California.

VIDEO TESTIMONIALS

Video-taped testimonials and music videos of male, female, and children singers who have trained with Thomas Appell are available for viewing at the VDP Publishing website **www.vocalinstruction.com.** Check them out!

126